Destination: Holyoke

ISBN-13: 978-0-9790773-0-2
ISBN-10: 0-9790773-0-3

Destination: Holyoke

Immigration and Migration to Holyoke

Kate Navarra Thibodeau

Wistariahurst Museum

"Give me your tired, your poor,
Your huddled masses, yearning to breathe free,
The wretched refuse of your teeming shore,
Send these, the homeless, tempest-tost, to me:
I lift my lamp beside the golden door."
                    - Emma Lazarus; inscription on the Statue of Liberty

"The history of Holyoke is the history of Massachusetts
industrialism and all its social consequences."
                    – Constance McLaughlin Green

"Holyokers possess an indefinable quality of open heartedness,
frankness and friendliness that sets them apart from peoples of
any other city."
                    – Howard Conant

Acknowledgements

Holyoke, Massachusetts no doubt has a history. But through the years of researching Holyoke's history and looking through the window at Holyoke's past, it occurred to me that the family histories and stories of businesses and mills in Holyoke make up its history. Visitors to Wistariahurst learn the history of the Skinner Family within the context of the city's history, but the stories of the individuals who make up the mosaic of Holyoke have not been heard except around the dinner table, in local restaurants, and in obituaries. It is time to put photographs and words together with the voices of Holyoke's past and present to tell Holyoke's history. While the following pages are in no way a comprehensive history of Holyoke, it is my hope that they will inspire families, friends and Holyokers around the country to talk about their own history and the history of this city.

This book could not have been put together without the diligent research of Constance McLaughlin Green, who wrote the first and most comprehensive history of Holyoke. Daniel Czitrom began what can be called the introduction to this story in the 1980s with the public history exhibit entitled "The Hidden Holyoke: A Cityscape and its People," along with Carlos Vega and Bill Ravanesi. While their experiences researching and installing the exhibit have inspired me, there needed to be more done to unveil Holyoke's story for the public. I hope this book takes their scholarship a step further.

Sarah Campbell, Curator of the Holyoke Public Library History Room, has searched through her records with me for immigrants' and migrants' stories. That collection has also contributed many photos to the history within these pages. Understanding deadlines, she has helped immensely in getting this publication to its public. Theodore Belsky, who has contributed greatly to the collections of oral histories in the Pioneer Valley, has thrilled me with access to these oral histories, of which this book contains a wealth of stories. Mara Dodge has allowed me to use many of her sources for information on strikes and the labor movement in Holyoke and I thank her. The Transcript-Telegram has provided some of the photos and much of the information, and I thank that institution greatly.

The Massachusetts Foundation for the Humanities provided funding for me to do research on the immigration and migration to Holyoke, and without institutions who support local history, information would be much harder to disperse. The Wistariahurst Museum Association Inc., Friends of Wistariahurst Museum, have also provided funding for the production of *Destination Holyoke*.

Jill Hodnicki has challenged many Holyokers to learn about the history around them, through the architecture of the houses and mill buildings, headstones, and family histories. I hope she continues to challenge me and many other Holyokers. I thank her, Charlie Lotspeich at Holyoke Heritage State Park, and Phyllis

Woolf all who reviewed earlier editions, for their exuberant interest and input in the following pages. When the museum launched a new program that collected digital images of Holyoke family histories, no one knew we would find the heart of the city. I thank the people who have contributed to the collection of family histories in photos and other documents now housed at Wistariahurst, especially Francis Wagner, Janice Walker, Pauline Giusti Walton, Marie Doherty, Shirley Morrison, Angela Conway and the Hampson Family. Some of their stories are in the following pages. Thank you to all Holyokers for making the story of this city as amazing as it is.

A special thanks to Carol Constant and Melissa Boisselle for their continued support and refreshing views on the history of Holyoke. Thanks also go to my husband and family, and my extended family - Holyoke.

While some immigrants and migrants have moved on from Holyoke, others have stayed for many generations. Other Holyokers have lived in the city for just a few years. This book is for anyone who identifies with Holyoke in their hearts.

Kate Navarra Thibodeau, Curator
Wistariahurst Museum
Holyoke, 2006

Contents

By the late 1800s, Holyoke was firmly established as an industrial center based on its paper and textile manufacturing. This photograph was taken on High Street, between Dwight and Lyman Streets. Photograph courtesy of the Wistariahurst Museum Archives.

Destination Holyoke

"…we *all* are in this strange country"

By the 1880s, Holyoke, known as The Paper City, was booming with industry. Without the help of immigrants and migrants, it would not have become a successful industrial center. It was a city of newcomers. Holyoke's population doubled between the years 1870 and 1880, and by 1890, the population was consistently over 50% foreign born. Over 150 years, many different people came to work in Holyoke and made the city their home. As each group of people arrived – Irish, French Canadians, Italians, Germans, Poles and Puerto Ricans – they adjusted to their new lives in the city and joined the competition for jobs and housing.

Most European immigrants came to America by boat with nothing but the clothes on their backs, possibly a trunk, and a small amount of money stashed carefully away. Some did not know English and most had little or no formal education. During the 1700s and 1800s, immigrants from overseas traveled in horrific conditions. A character in *The Parish on the Hill* by Mary Doyle Curran recounts, "The boat he sailed on was … a cattle boat, and he was quartered with cattle. The voyage took four weeks. He arrived in America hatless and shoeless, smelling of cattle dung."

At entry points to America like Ellis Island, men were separated from women and children. Officials asked thirty-two basic questions concerning name, age, country or city of origin, occupation, literacy, amount of money they carried and their final destination. Immigrants waited in long lines for a medical examination and the possibility of detainment in cells. Holyoke was one gateway city for immigrants looking for opportunity and the American Dream.

Immigrants from the German steamship *Princess Irene* disembarked at the West Side Manhattan pier in 1911. Photograph courtesy of Holyoke Heritage State Park.

The Connecticut River was an important source of food and livelihood for the Native Americans in the valley, and would later provide much needed water power for the mills of Holyoke. Photograph courtesy of Wistariahurst Museum Archives.

Before the area was settled by Europeans, Holyoke was the dividing line between the Agawam and the Nonotuck Indians. The territory of the Agawam Indians ran from Enfield, Connecticut to Holyoke. The Nonotuck Indians settled Holyoke and extended north into Deerfield. Both were independent tribes of the Algonquin Indian Nation, who lived on the east coast of America. Two Indian camps were known to be located in Holyoke. The largest settlement was located in the area west of Northampton Street, between Easthampton Road and Cherry Street. The second and smaller camp was located near Hitchcock

Street. The first Europeans settled the area when William Pynchon came to Springfield in 1636. With that, the European Americans gradually expanded up the Connecticut River Valley. Captain Rowland Thomas and Captain Elizur Holyoke were two of the many who explored the area. After King Phillip's War ended in 1676, there was a period of peace between white settlers and Native Americans. About three decades passed until the French and Indian War, and the local raid on Deerfield in 1704. As a result of the steady influx of white settlers, the Native Americans that fished and smoked shad along the nearby Connecticut River generally withdrew from the area.

In 1786, the third or northern part of Springfield was officially made into Ireland Parish, now known as Holyoke. Ireland Parish was named because John Riley, a Protestant Irishman, had settled the area in the 1600s. Other early settlers included Benjamin Ball and Captain John Miller. Ireland Parish was a farming village that utilized the rich land near the waterfalls on the western bank of the Connecticut River to grow hay, corn, rye, potatoes and oats. Farmers produced enough to meet their needs and a surplus which they sold at markets in Northampton and Springfield. The first attempt to develop this area was in 1792 when a group called "Proprietors of the Locks and Canals" on the Connecticut River completed the construction of a navigable canal around the South Hadley Falls. Though the construction did little to disturb Ireland Parish, the amount of merchandise that was able to be shipped north of Hadley Falls increased tremendously.

Land in Ireland Parish was mostly used for agriculture, but there were a few production mills. A small cotton mill, at the time valued at nearly $60,000, which employed less than 70 people, was using water power as early as 1845. Like the Native Americans before them, however, most of Ireland Parish's residents viewed the Connecticut River as a source of salmon and shad rather than power. Fish ran the river each spring and horses were often seen by the river waiting while farmers fished at the falls to supplement their diet of mostly grain and vegetables.

Change came in the late 1840s as settlers moved in, New England's roads developed, and the Western Massachusetts Railroad extended up the Connecticut River to Springfield. Later on, the Northampton Railroad Company merged with the Greenfield and Northampton line, which formed the Connecticut River Railroad. Besides the cotton mill, Ireland Parish had a grist mill, a tannery, a clock maker, a quarry, two physicians, a shoemaker, tailor, wheelwright, painter, blacksmith, one school, two churches and a tavern.

In 1846 and 1847, George Ewing, an agent for the Boston Associates, persuaded the reluctant farmers of the Ireland Parish to sell their land for the purposes of building a planned city. A group of investors from Boston Associates purchased land in Ireland Parish and planned to build a canal system that would provide

Immigrants arriving through Ellis Island were carefully tagged with their names and the steamship upon which they arrived. Some of the immigrants to Holyoke in this photo are still wearing their tags. Photograph courtesy of the Wistariahurst Museum Archives.

power for dozens of mills. The Boston Associates already held large investments in 22 cotton mills in cities such as Lowell and Chicopee. They saw opportunity in the Connecticut River when they measured in 1847 that at its driest time of the year, the water flow could produce 30,000 horsepower, enough for 550 mill powers. At the time, large mills used less than 5 mill powers. They planned this site

The first wooden dam was built by the Hadley Falls Company in 1847. Photograph courtesy of the Wistariahurst Museum Archives.

The more sturdy dam was built out of stone in front of the old wooden dam, c. late 1890s. Photograph courtesy of the Wistariahurst Museum Archives.

for an industrial city and because of its location on the fertile Connecticut River, agricultural products could be used as raw materials for factories and their laborers.

Engineers, who had previously surveyed the land, returned to map locations for the dam, the canals, mill sites, streets, boarding houses, and to change the routing and grading of the Connecticut River Railroad tracks where they cut through the land. Two South Hadley mills, the Glasgow Company and the Carew

Manufacturing Company, were contracted for water rights. The Holyoke mills would use their power supplied to the transportation canal, controlled by the Hadley Falls Company, via a short connecting canal cut through the eastern portion of the dam.

By 1847, the grand canal system was designed. Irish laborers provided the first immigrant work force, having arrived in 1847 to construct the new dam and mill buildings. The Hadley Falls Company began construction of Holyoke's first wooden dam in 1847. The city streets were laid out in relation to the canal system in a grid pattern. In addition, parks and other areas for recreation were planned.

Work had to be suspended for a time in January 1848 because of a strike among the Irish laborers at having their pay cut from 75 cents to 70 cents a day. Despite a brief display of violence the men were soon persuaded to return peacefully to work by the arrival of militiamen from Northampton and the counsel of the Catholic priest from Springfield who hurried to the scene.

The dam was completed and one day in November of 1848 at 10 AM, the gates of the newly constructed dam were closed and the reservoir began to rise. At 3:26 PM, the dam was swept away with the now famous words "Dam gone to hell by way of Willimansett." A second dam, built with an apron for additional support, was started in 1849 and took seven months to complete.

The Hadley Falls Company employed men in construction from many different backgrounds.

Parson's Paper, shown here in the background, was the first paper mill built in Holyoke. The foreground construction is the first level canal in c. 1850s. Photograph courtesy of the Wistariahurst Museum Archives.

From 1849 to 1853, there were a total of 449 men employed from the countries of Ireland, Scotland, England, Canada, New Brunswick, and Nova Scotia, while 388 men came from within the state of Massachusetts.

Irish immigrants to Holyoke were part of an exodus to America that began in the 1820s, but by the 1850s, the number grew to almost one million. The hardships in Ireland of the potato famines of 1822, 1831, 1835, 1837, 1842 and 1846 were almost entirely confined to the Irish laboring population in Great Britain. Although tens of thousands of Irish began emigrating after the 1820s, not everyone wanted to go to England and an even smaller number were able to go directly to America. But potato famine was not the sole reason the Irish left their native land. Irish immigrants were seeking religious freedom, escaping the exploitation of British rule, tax collectors and the enforced payment of tithe to a church in whose doctrine they did not believe. In Great Britain, the Act of Union (1801) had made it difficult for manufacturers in Ireland to compete with the more developed factories of Great Britain. The Irish could not survive in their own country with an exploding population and diminishing work opportunities. The British government established a police force that allowed wider enforcement of laws regarding landlord efforts to clear estates and collect rents. Destitute as small tenant farmers were in the countryside of Great Britain, if they chose not to leave, they could only continue their status quo, hoping that epidemics and starvation would pass them by.

The Irish came from simple agricultural backgrounds and when they arrived at America's shores, they were plunged into an impersonal and industrial economy. Emigration from Ireland never again reached famine peaks, but it continued to be heavy and steady throughout the last half of the 1800s. From 1870 to 1900, more than 1.5 million Irish entered the United States.

Irish immigrants, from the time they began to arrive in large numbers, were distrusted by established Americans. The Irish were thought to be an "inferior race" because they were so poor they had to sell their labor. They were also predominantly Catholic, which was a religion thought to be based on superstition and controlled by The Pope who demanded absolute loyalty. Irish immigrants were also suspected of reserving their loyalties for the Irish struggle for independence from England. Some in America thought they might never put America first and were suspicious of their enclaves communities, living according to the social patterns of their homeland. Some business owners and many residents of the area regarded Irish laborers, who had begun to arrive in the small hill towns around Holyoke as "stupid and dirty, superstitious and untrustworthy, diseased and in despair. They were viewed as beggars and thieves." When the impoverished Irish first found work, they often slept in a barn or constructed shanties.

With so much construction going on in the 1850s, laborers were in heavy demand. Irish immigrants

As industry grew in Holyoke, so did its population. These Holyoke residents watch the preparation of the riverbed for the construction of the stone dam, c. late 1880s. Photograph courtesy of the Wistariahurst Museum Archives.

provided man hours for this rugged and dangerous work. Though the canal was only partly granite, some men were killed shifting huge blocks of granite from place to place when fixing the canal walls. For example, the Transcript Telegram reported on February 4, 1848, two workers were killed, one in a slide of earth, the other after falling while working on the railroad.

Although far from their native land, Irish emigrants, particularly women, kept in touch with their families back home in Ireland. Although they were at the lowest rung of the socioeconomic ladder, Irish workers managed to send almost 60 million dollars to Ireland in bank drafts and money orders over a 13 year period (1848-1861). Countless letters contained many more unrecorded dollars.

The Hadley Falls Company went bankrupt in 1857 and its assets were purchased by John Chase and his business partners in 1859, renaming the company Holyoke Water Power Company. At the same time, there existed in Ireland Parish 19 craft based shops like brick makers, shoemakers, harness makers, black smiths, coppersmiths and others who conducted small, independent enterprises.

With the slow and steady growth in population and industrialization, there were a few dramatic and dangerous happenings. In 1855, the town's newspaper, the Weekly Mirror, ran a dramatic story of a rescue on the Connecticut River. "On Monday evening Holyoke was the scene of a fearful accident, which, however, was not attended with serious results. As David Gleason, Timothy Crowly and John Barry were crossing the river above the dam in a small boat one of the row-locks broke…and the boat was carried over the dam about midway of the river." The boat sank but the Irishmen aboard hung onto rocks. Several bystanders sounded an alarm. As it was getting dark, bonfires were lit on both sides of the river to let the water logged men know help was on its way. A man named Joseph Ely took command of a flat-bottomed boat and with his brothers Samuel and Austin, and several others to rescue the men. Within 25 minutes, the boat returned with the wet and frightened men safe and sound. The paper reported the air on both sides of the river "rung with cheers."

The Holyoke Water Power Company, employing mostly Irish immigrants, began construction on a new and even stronger stone dam in the 1890s and finished in 1900. At the same time, even more mill sites were being sold and mills constructed. Even by the 1870s, Holyoke was no longer the agricultural backwater it had been before 1847. The population had increased from 3,245 in 1850 to 10,733 in 1870 and it was well on its way to becoming the Paper City. Eleven paper mills employed more than 1,000 workers producing tissue, book, collar and the fine white writing paper that would make the city famous.

Some Irish immigrants, however, did not work in the mills. Martin P. Conway was born in Ireland in 1858, but immigrated to America when he was 7 years old. He was a dealer in merchandise of pianos, organs, general musical items at 305 High Street. He served as Alderman for two terms, the last being president of the Board. He was also a Water Commissioner for three years and chairman two of those years.

Daniel J. O'Connell, founder of the construction firm Daniel J. O'Connell's Sons Construction Company, arrived in Holyoke from Ireland in 1847 at the age of 14. He first worked as a water boy for the construction team of the original Holyoke dam. He moved on to the job of barn boss for the Hadley Falls Company's horse teams. From there he went into business for himself as a truck man having materials for hire, then worked for the city as a superintendent of streets. In the 1880s, he launched the construction company which was passed on to his six sons. Their descendants continue the business today.

Another shrewd young Irishman, Michael Conners, who came to Holyoke in 1888 from Ireland, launched a small cigar business selling Kaffir cigars to local saloon-keepers. He eventually served as Alderman for Ward Three, when he used his position to benefit his business. Saloon keepers who wanted licenses were expected to buy at least 100,000 Kaffir cigars at $60 per thousand. This corruption was ended in 1896 and new policies were established so that there could be no benefit for someone in the Alderman position in the city.

Lucien Chretian was born in Quebec province, Canada, in 1874. Photograph courtesy of Marie T. Doherty.

French Canadians who arrived in Holyoke during the 1870s and the 1880s were the second largest immigrant group. French Canadians traveled south to New England individually or in small family groups. Except for the relatively small number who fled Quebec because of the Patriote Rebellion of the 1830s, most immigrants sought improvement to their lives. Thousands of Canadians left Quebec in the years following the British conquest, settling in other Canadian provinces and throughout the United States. The available cultivatable land could not expand with the population growth in Canada. In addition, French Canadians were reluctant to adopt modern farm technologies, leading to smaller harvests and an agricultural depression. American manufacturers also paid their workers more than Canadian manufacturers. By the late 1800s, more than 300,000 French Canadians had moved to New England.

Those who crossed the Canadian border to come to America first sent back enthusiastic accounts of America along with more money than the family at home had ever seen. Most headed for American cities and towns where relatives or friends had preceded them and where they had reason to believe they could find work. Holyoke became one of those cities.

The Holyoke Transcript Telegram of April 5, 1873 reported: "Frenchmen are coming into town 'thicker and faster and more of 'em' according to the officer stationed at the Connecticut Railroad depot who said there were fresh arrivals with every train." The French Canadian population in Holyoke increased from 17% to 28% between 1870 and 1880.

The spring of 1879 brought into Massachusetts another great wave of French Canadians immigrants, lured by rumors of abundant jobs in the mills. The Transcript-Telegram on March 29, 1879 described the scene in Holyoke: "They come with all their worldly goods packed in boxes and bundles and the gents' room at the Connecticut Railroad depot is packed with their effects till it looks like a wholesale warehouse. Leaving the bulk of articles at the depot, they start out with their arms full of bundles to find a place to stop. Some have friends or relatives here. Many have spent their last cent to get here, expecting to find plenty of work on their arrival......"

Many French Canadians took skilled work in the textile mills of Holyoke, while others worked in construction. For example, Lucien Chretian, born in Quebec, immigrated to Holyoke in 1891 and worked for both the Lyman and Farr Alpaca Mills. Chretian eventually became a contractor of buildings in Holyoke. He built the Strathmore Apartments, the Lotus building, erected in 1912, the Cambria building in 1915, the Colonial building in 1916, and the Comodore just one year later.

Blanch Manuello, a French Canadian who later worked in the Skinner Silk Mills, remembered that "South Holyoke was mostly all French. My grandfather came over first. Then my grandmother, mother and father came after. Mother cried. My father told her when they had 10,000 francs they could go back. That was only $35 American, but they never went back..."

A smaller but important group who settled in Holyoke beginning in the 1860s were German families. The 1830s in Germany struggled with cholera epidemics, popular uprisings and rumors of revolution and war. At the same time, the lands of America, they noted, were not burdened by the heavy taxes

Ella Siegert stands between her parents Julius and Frederica Siegert. Ella was born in Holyoke but her parents immigrated from Germany. After high school, Ella worked in the Germania Mills. Photograph courtesy of Janice Walker.

which took the cash profits of Ahr Valley farmers. The textile workers from the Rhineland and Saxony were trained in hand weaving and had experience in German textile markets. Germany's transition to machine production caused a decrease in the need for textile workers. Also, the political regimentation of the Bismarck national program deprived German citizens of their freedom. Working German families used their savings to purchase homes in the United States.

German immigrants in Holyoke settled in South Holyoke, which was formerly inhabited by French Canadians, and survived in a community already divided along ethnic and religious lines. August and Hermann

Stursberg, owners of woolen mills in Germany, bought half interest in the Germania Mills in Holyoke. Unlike the Irish who preceded them, German spinners and weavers found an easy niche in Holyoke because the Stursberg brothers brought them to Holyoke for work and helped them make a home in South Holyoke.

The German population was growing in Holyoke so rapidly that in 1874 a Transcript-Telegram news item stated the city clerk, E.A. Ramsay, was taking a course in German so he could spell the German names correctly for his job.

Polish immigration to Holyoke began after the close of the American Civil War and the end of the 1863 Polish Revolt for independence. Polish immigrants to Holyoke were largely young adults, either single, or married with children too young to work. The one sure place Polish immigrants could find work was the Lyman Cotton Mills. For example, Anthony Symasko was born in Poland in 1877. He came to America when he was 16 years old to work on a farm in Deerfield, Massachusetts. In 1895, he came to Holyoke to do odd jobs like working in a liquor store and a café. It was 1905 when he started his own undertaking business, established on 134 High Street.

Italians first came to Holyoke in the late 1880s. Records show many Italians established confectionery and fruit stores between 1882 and 1900. They were owned by Rigali, Musante, Campagna, Buglia, Equi, Luchini, and Marano. These stores were located on High or Main Street. Although the Italian community was scattered throughout the city, for a certain number of years, a large number of the Italians who did not live near their stores lived on Bond Street, an area known as "Little Italy." The Mazzolini Family immigrated to Holyoke and lived on 66 Brookline Avenue. Joseph Mazzolini came in 1892 and worked at Caesar Equi confectionery store which boasted "Bananas a Specialty." His brother August joined him in 1905 and together they opened up a new store.

Frank J. Equi owned a coffee and sandwich shop on Main Street and was in the business for 80 years. He began working at the shop with his father when he was 16 years old. In 1975, he sold the business to Bernard Cawley of Feeding Hills who continued the restaurant business.

Frank Giusti was born in Fornaci de Barga, Italy, in 1898 and immigrated to America at the age of ten. He and his parents settled in Holyoke along with other families from the same area of Italy. Eventually he opened a fruit and confectionery store at the corner of Pleasant and Hampden Street. He always

Frank Giusti. Photograph courtesy of Pauline Giusti Walton.

had an interest in photography. Along with owning the store, he started working as a photographer for the Springfield newspapers. Because of an interest in photography, he moved next door to 477 Pleasant Street and opened up Giusti's Camera Shop, which was in business for 29 years. He did commercial photography. Dr. John Fitzgibbons, a dentist who was known internationally for his work with cleft palate patients, hired Giusti to photograph his patients before and after appliances were made for them. He traveled to conferences throughout the country with the dentist. Giusti also photographed Belle Skinner's musical instrument collection. He died in 1950 at the age of 52.

Portuguese immigrants first arrived in Holyoke in the early 1900s, drawn by work in the textile mills, and to escape what many felt was an oppressive military draft law in Portugal. Some worked at Mackintosh and Sons Company, Farr Alpaca and at the American Thread Company.

Olga Maria Amaral, born in Portugal, moved to Holyoke in 1967 at the age of 12. She noted how different the two cultures were: "The Portuguese people I found here did not think [education] was so important. The Portuguese people here thought that working in a factory was enough. That, for me, was a shock. The culture shock I had with the Portuguese in America was for me a bigger shock than the one I had with Americans."

Mary Doyle Curran's character in *Parish on the Hill* reflects that as "… foreigners we all are in this strange country. Its little enough any of us understand about it except that its swelling like a great balloon, and who is to prevent its bursting into a thousand pieces, one piece dividing against another if we do not make peace with one another."

From the 1880s forward many laws limiting immagration were enacted. The strict immigration laws included the Chinese Exclusion Act of 1882, which restricted all Chinese immigration. It also levied a tax of 50 cents per immigrant and made several categories of immigrants, like lunatics, ineligible to enter America. In 1892, Ellis Island opened and was able to monitor and apply these immigration acts as they changed throughout the next 100 years. By 1921, the Quota Act was created to limit annual European immigration to 3% of the number of the nationality group in the United State in 1910. In 1943, the Chinese Exclusion Act was repealed. Just a decade later, the Internal Security Act banned admission to America by any immigrant who may be a Communist. In 1952, the McCarran Walter Immigration Act, passed over President Harry Truman's veto, affirmed the national-origins quota system of 1924 and limited the total annual immigration to one-sixth of 1% of the population of the continental United States in 1920. Later immigration laws were enacted to prevent certain groups from entering America. Operation Wetback in 1954 forced the return of thousands of illegal aliens to Mexico. In 1956, the Hungarian Revolution was crushed by the Soviets, but before it totally failed, refugees in numbers of almost three hundred thousands came to the United States by 1960. From 1950 to 1960, the United States welcomed immigrants from Germany, Italy, Holland, the United Kingdom, Japan, Canada and Mexico. In 1965, the Immigration and Nationality Act Amendments abolished the system of national origin quotas. Since then, peoples from many countries have immigrated unrestricted. Puerto Rican migration to the United States was also part of a larger national pattern of replacement migration from the Western Hemisphere. Puerto Ricans filled the labor demand caused by the earlier restriction of immigrants from Asia and Europe.

Holyoke was becoming more than just an industrial city in the mid-1900s. Her borders held in a mosaic of cultures and heritages, as shown in store fronts along many streets downtown. Photograph courtesy of the Wistariahurst Museum Archives.

In 1940s Holyoke, the streets downtown were full of first, second or third generation immigrants. Anita Marcotte Healey, French Canadian, remembered how "Main Street was a hustle and bustle place with a good ethnic mixture of businesses- there was a Greek, a Jew, French and Polish. The Irish were mostly up the hill and the Germans on Park Street."

Carlos Vega, Director of Nueva Esperanza, Inc., reminds us that "Holyoke has always been a city where immigrants came to live and work, it was built just for that reason." Puerto Rico was a colony of Spain until 1898, when in the Spanish American War, the United States was awarded all of Spain's colonies. The Jones Act of 1917 made Puerto Ricans citizens of the United States. While earlier European immigrants entered America by boat, Puerto Ricans boarded Pan Am airplanes and had no need to pass through

The Robles Family, Antonio, Abimeal, Maria and Edgar, pictured in 1979. Photograph courtesy of the Holyoke Public Library History Room.

immigration, as they were American citizens. There were three waves of Puerto Rican migration to main land America. The first began in the late 1940s and 1950s. At the end of World War II, the United States government promised to help veterans get an education and purchase homes with the GI Bill. In general, the nation was seeing veterans attending college rather than returning to work in the mills. Also the Puerto Rican agricultural economy was deteriorating and farmers migrated to America for jobs in tobacco fields. They worked seasonally as farm workers and some worked in the mills.

The second wave of migration was caused by a 1968 economic recession on the Island of Puerto Rico, resulting in an influx of Puerto Ricans to the Pioneer Valley seeking employment in the local tobacco fields. Puerto Ricans were attracted to their island cities for industrial jobs and abandoned their farms. However, Puerto Rico lacked an urban industrial economy that could absorb a mushrooming population. Puerto Ricans came to find jobs. Domingo Perez moved to Holyoke in 1956. He said "We arrived on a Sunday and by Monday we were working, and in two weeks I found another job in a factory." In the 1980s, Domingo managed 70 apartments he owned in Holyoke. He and his wife Escolastica were able to succeed in their new hometown. Domingo said it was easy to find work, and they did not need to know the language in the factories, as was the case with earlier immigrants from Poland and Germany, "there were other people that knew it [what to do] and helped us when we need it." Herminio Malave came to Holyoke in 1968 from Salinas, Puerto Rico, where he was an unemployed cane-cutter. In Holyoke, he "came Sunday, I worked Monday," washing fabric at Pioneer Valley Finishing Company.

The last wave of Puerto Ricans migrated to mainland America in the 1980s and 1990s. About 4,500 people from Puerto Rico came within a matter of 3-4 years. This smaller group of migrants was able to find jobs as bilingual service providers, in health and human services and in educational fields. The continuing deterioration of Puerto Rico's economy meant less employment possibilities. In addition, public assistance benefits to help with the transition made it possible for many Puerto Ricans to migrate to the mainland. However, this wave of Puerto Rican migrants contained a number of Puerto Rican college graduates who were unable to find a job on the island due to lack of work experience and opportunities.

Initially, many Puerto Ricans settled in poorer urban neighborhoods near tobacco fields in Hartford, Connecticut and Springfield. President Lyndon B. Johnson's "urban renewal" meant that cities could receive money to rehabilitate certain areas of the city. Thus, Springfield demolished housing and forced Puerto Ricans out of the north end. They moved to Holyoke, where they found inexpensive tenement housing in the Flats and jobs in the factories. Unlike earlier immigrant groups which came to Holyoke during periods of expanding population and economy, Puerto Ricans migrated to Holyoke when industrial jobs were harder to find. By the 1980s, there were four downtown neighborhoods inhabited by mostly Puerto Ricans. Today, Holyoke's population is 41% Latino; of that 99% are Puerto Rican.

Esther Sotolongos, born in Puerto Rico, points out that "people from Europe are not citizens. But we [Puerto Ricans] are. We're not foreigners. We're citizens."

Puerto Ricans, like the groups who came to Holyoke before them, relied on the people around them for support. No matter what ethnicity, families and neighbors built their lives and relationships in Holyoke. Anna Sullivan, a longtime Holyoke activist, remembers a city filled with newcomers: "Everybody had huge families. These were the days, you

Children from different backgrounds come together in school in the 1970s. Photograph courtesy of the Holyoke Public Library History Room.

know. Those women were marvelous. They never went to hospitals, you know, never went to a hospital for a baby. But they all helped one another, always. If Mrs. Murphy was having a baby, why, everybody done something. Either a pot of soup went one day or somebody else brought a loaf of bread and clothes, they always got together and made and shared, they used to get together. Also they used to get together to make clothes for the kiddos at Brightside. These women had time, they were always busy. Of course, we never had anything from the bakery. And doctors were few and far between and very seldom…. You never got to a doctor unless you were dying. You didn't have the money."

Population Make Up in Holyoke, 1850-2000

Year	Total Pop.	Native Born	Puerto Rico	Foreign Born	Ireland	French Canada	Britain	France	Germany	Poland	Italy
1850	3,245				1,657	40	292				
1860	4,497	2,623									
1870	10,733	5,257		5,490	2,850	1,731	531		299		
1880	21,915	4,368		10,915	4,241	4,902	1,085		509		
1890	35,637	6,064		17,068	5,993	7,046	1,156	30	1,455	73	81
1900	45,712	7,771		18,892	5,650	6,991	2,945	108	1,602	1,126	132
1910	57,730	34,492		23,238	5,246	8,035	1,365	391	1,565		368
1920	63,655	39,776		20,255	4,261	5,806	1,249	428	1,011	2,701	368
1930	56,537	40,706		15,831	7,872	7,328	1,028	274	910	4,623	473
1940	53,750	38,546		12,067	2,393	3,072	756	177	663	2,020	316
1950	54,661	39,365		9,464	1,671	2,867	546	144	501	1,669	280
1960	52,689	45,313		7,304	Not reported..						
1970	50,051	44,345		4,038	574	1,071	349	44	272	900	93
1980	44,678	41,506	5,808	3,172	170	850	156	42	205	552	72
1990	43,704	41,241	13,592	2,463	147	386	19	20	112	564	64
2000	39,838		16,493	1,086							

Data complied from United States Census Records and City of Holyoke Directories.

When investors began to build an industrial city, there was a massive flow of immigrants into Ireland Parish, established as the City of Holyoke in 1873. Photograph courtesy of the Wistariahurst Museum Archives.

Holyoke's Neighborhoods

"If you lived in a tenement block there'd probably be an Irish, a French-Canadian, and probably a couple of Germans, a Jew or two further down below, a Belgian on the first floor..."

Ireland Parish was the name given to the third, or north, parish when it was set off from West Springfield. As early as 1684, Ireland native John Riley purchased 16 acres of land in this new area and by 1720 a major division of lots was made in what would eventually become the town of Holyoke. In 1831 Ireland Parish, there were 130 homes. In 1847, when the dam and canals were being constructed, there was a massive flow of immigrants into a town which needed their labor but was not prepared to provide for them. As immigrant groups came for economic opportunity, they created enclave communities built around the mills where they worked and their places of worship.

The Patch, part of what would later become Ward 4, was the area between Hampden Street and Prospect Park, near the river just above the dam. The first Irish who settled in the Patch were squatters on Holyoke Water Power Company land. When the dam was being built in the 1850s, it was customary for new arrivals to construct a shelter. These shelters were crude, made of boards and dug out holes in the ground, comprising one room and a loft. Some even took borders who slept in a loft on straw. These shanties had no large windows for ventilation and plumbing was virtually nonexistent. Sewers were not extended to the Patch until 1873. Families were later allowed use of the land in the Patch for $3 per week.

The dominant feature in the foreground of this 1876 photograph is the row houses that Lyman Cotton Mills built for their workers. Photograph courtesy of the Holyoke Public Library History Room.

Most families raised pigs, goats, chickens, and vegetables, and fished the Connecticut River for food.. Wood was used for heating more commonly than coal and many cut their own or salvaged wood from the river. It was often crowded in the shanties. A reporter from the Holyoke Transcript-Telegram wrote in 1879: "I was stopped at one of the shanties…first, the man and woman came out the door, then six children….then six boarders… then a cow….then a sow and six pigs came out, all from the same door….."

Frenchville was the area where French Canadians arrived and settled in the 1850s near the dam in Ward 4 and the Lyman Cotton Mills. An invisible line was drawn separating the Irish Patch from Frenchville. Crossing the line was a dangerous thing to do. William McFadden, who came to Holyoke as an infant with his Canadian parents said "I was brought up on the toughest street in the city; it was just like the Bowery in New York. Union Street. They called it Canada Hill in those days. All French people there. It was awful rough. The Irishmen couldn't come down below High Street. If the Frenchmen go up the hill there'd be a fight. I was half and half, so I was getting along good. But it was a very tough neighborhood."

Known today as South Holyoke, Tigertown took its name from the rough Irishmen who located there in the late 1850s to work in the Holyoke Paper mills or the nearby brickyard. Tigertown was the area between the second and third level canals furthest from the dam. By the 1870s, Tigertown's borders held Polish, German and French Canadian inhabitants, but they did not mingle. Most Germans worked at the Germania Woolen Mills in South Holyoke, where they later established a culturally distinct neighborhood that set them apart from the city's other ethnic groups.

The Highlands around Pleasant Street were originally called "Manchester Grounds," named after Manchester, New Hampshire by a group of capitalists from that town who bought this large tract of land to develop streets and homes. When they were not successful, the name was dropped, and the area became known as the Highlands. Manufacturing families like the Dwights, Chases, Townes, Toepferts, Steigers and Whitings built beautiful homes there. These neighborhoods are largely intact today.

The Flats, or Ward 1, was within the original planned industrial city. The Hadley Falls Company bought all the land from farmers prior to building the Holyoke dam. A small group of Irish immigrants lived in the Flats and were replaced by French Canadians when they moved into town. After a series of tenement fires in the 1970s, much of the flats have been developed into two-family homes.

Ward 4 has been the only name for an area bounded by the Connecticut River to the north, first level canal to the east, Dwight Street to the south and the Muller Bridge to the west area settled mostly by the Polish. The Polish community in Holyoke extended to Chicopee as opportunities opened in the various textile mills there.

20

A view of The Highlands, Holyoke, Massachusetts, c. 1888. Photograph courtesy of the Wistariahurst Museum Archives.

The influx of the Polish immigrants stopped around 1914 at the outbreak of World War I. High Street from Hampden Street north to the river was referred to as "Polish Avenue," which had over 70 businesses owned by Poles. Amid the decaying tenements, togetherness was a more important aspect of life than moving to a more fashionable part of town. By 1895, Polish settlements in Holyoke contained more than 300 residents. They later settled in Ward 4, formerly the home of many French Canadians.

Dorothy Hamel, an Irish descendant, recalls "Ward 4 was mostly mill hands. Irish and French, they didn't get along, but I don't know why…each thought they were better than the other. [There were] mostly French in Ward 2. The Polish came into Ward 4 and the Irish moved out and up the hill. The Polish fixed up the neighborhood…."

Companies built tenement houses for their workers. Often the backyards were small and the rooms were big and cold. This is the housing for the Hadley Thread Mills on Lyman Street, originally built in the mid 1800s. Photograph courtesy of the Wistariahurst Museum Archives.

Children on a stoop in the tenement blocks of Holyoke. Photograph courtesy of the Wistariahurst Museum Archives.

Hadley Thread Mills housing on Lyman and Grover Street, originally built in the mid 1800s. Photograph courtesy of the Holyoke Public Library History Room.

Squalid living conditions contributed to the severe cholera and dysentery epidemic in 1849. Sanitation provided was next to nothing; and refrigeration was unknown. Men, women and children died by the dozens. Dr. Lawson A. Long, a New York physician stationed in Holyoke in 1849 reported that cholera raged in the Patch for six weeks. Eight to fifteen people succumbed daily, with 300 dead in six weeks.

In the last stages of cholera, the skin becomes shrunken and shriveled, indicative of the lack of fluid in the tissue. Doctor Long rolled up the gravely ill body in hot wet blankets and placed a large feather mattress over the body and head. Five hours later, the victims' feet were warm, their face flushed and the blankets were dry! After being given brandy and ammonia, the victim started to breathe. From this there were reports of complete recovery.

Poverty was rampant in 1873. On any given day at the city's fruit and vegetable stands, wrote the Transcript Telegram's editor, one could see "a drove of poverty stricken children, often girls, clad only in one or two ragged and dirty garments, down on their hands and knees in the gutters, greedily picking out of the mud and dirt and eating the bits of spoiled and decaying fruit which have been thrown out as worthless." Not all working class families suffered such hardship, but wage reductions in winters coupled with intermittent periods of unemployment placed serious economic pressures on the families of even the best paid workers.

The Board of Health was composed of the three town selectmen in 1856. They established rules for keeping alleys and streets free from garbage, cleaning outhouses, building sewers and drains. However, in 1870 and 1873, Holyoke experienced smallpox epidemics. Beginning with the workers employed in the rag rooms in the paper mills, the disease spread rapidly through town. "Pest houses" were built so the victims of the disease could be segregated. The dead were covered with quicklime and buried immediately. The Aldermen banned public entertainment of all kind. In 1880 the city established a full time Board of Health. New regulations required vaccination of all children, mill employees and school teachers, as well as rules for managing sanitation and garbage collection.

As time went on, the shanties disappeared and were replaced by long rows of red-brick tenements built by the mill owners. Some of these can still be seen in Holyoke today. In 1861, the Holyoke Transcript described a block of these company tenements in South Holyoke as "having a handsome front of pressed

Hadley Thread Mills housing, which were later restored as townhouses. Photograph courtesy of the Holyoke Public Library History Room.

brick, double circular windows, three stories high with French roof, and twenty-eight rooms with a dining room, pantries, a kitchen, with most of the rooms finished in oak graining…" As more people entered the city, people crowded into small, dark tenements, sometimes ten to twelve families in an apartment which was meant for two or three. Overcrowding, filth and lack of privacy compounded by a growing tendency to build multi-storied tenements and to construct more rear houses back to back with other buildings, thus encroaching further upon courts and alleys.

In 1875, the Massachusetts Bureau of Statistics and Labor reported that "Holyoke has more and worse large tenement houses than any manufacturing town of textile fabrics in the state, and built in such a manner that there is little means of escape in case of fire. The sanitary arrangements are imperfect and in many cases there is no provision made for carrying the slops from the sinks, but they are allowed to run wherever they can make their way. Portions of yards are covered with filth and green slime, and within twenty feet, people are living in basements of houses three feet below the level of the yard."

Congestion soon became a problem due to lack of good transportation within the city. The incorporation of the Holyoke Street Railway in 1884 relieved overcrowding in areas near mills by opening up new sections of the city to the working classes who built small houses in areas further from downtown.

There were many violent outbreaks in Ward 4 between the Poles and French Canadians. The press sided

High Street is the prominent road in this photograph surrounded by company mill tenements. This photo was taken from City Hall in 1876. Photograph courtesy of the Holyoke Public Library History Room.

with the French Canadians, who had achieved certain stability in Holyoke. Many Poles stayed in the city only long enough to accumulate wages to purchase farms in the fertile Connecticut River valley. This migration intensified when many Poles were laid off by the Lyman Mills in 1927.

Poles settled in the neighborhood around Lyman Mills, where they worked. All mill employees who had no families were expected to live in the boarding houses, where respectable housekeepers were to keep track of the boarders conduct, the doors to be closed at ten o'clock in the evening and the boarders not allowed to congregate on the front steps or sidewalk in front of their tenement.

Blanche Manuello, whose parents were immigrants and worked as weavers, remembered growing up in Holyoke. "If you lived in a tenement block there'd probably be an Irish, a French-Canadian, and probably

This photo is of the original horse car on its way to South Hadley Falls. Photograph courtesy of the Wistariahurst Museum Archives.

Lyman Mills housing. Photograph courtesy of the Holyoke Public Library History Room.

81 Bond Street apartments in 1927. Photograph courtesy of the Holyoke Public Library History Room.

a couple of Germans, a Jew or two further down below, a Belgian on the first floor. It just didn't matter. The only thing that mattered which I can remember the most is that no matter who you were or what nationality nobody worked on Sunday. And nobody would do laundry on Sunday."

In the mid 1900s, when Puerto Ricans migrated from other parts of the Connecticut Valley and Puerto Rico, the primary attraction of Holyoke was the availability of low-cost rental housing in the Flats area, between the first and second level canals. The predominant housing type was the three to five story brick structure, many constructed prior to 1900. The bulk of the Puerto Rican work force were engaged in seasonal labor in the tobacco industry.

The Battleship Block, built in 1911, once encompased the block of Canal, Bridge, Summer and Jackson Streets in South Holyoke. Today, there are only two parts of the block left. Photograph courtesy of the Holyoke Public Library History Room.

East Dwight Street tenement. Photograph courtesy of the Holyoke Public Library History Room.

The amazing dam and canal design of the Holyoke Water Power Company made the industrial efforts of mills in Holyoke a success. Photograph courtesy of the Wistariahurst Museum Archives.

Laboring in Holyoke's Industries

"We did not come to this country to starve."

Work opportunities in Holyoke's industries drew waves of immigrants from Europe, French Canada and migrants from Puerto Rico to make Holyoke their home. Companies that provided water and fuel, as well as logging companies, began before the paper and textile mills were built, all using water power to run their businesses. In 1873, there were 16 paper mills, 7 cotton mills, 3 woolen mills, 3 lumber mills and 2 machine shops. By 1880, half of Holyoke's work force labored in the growing textile mills, and six out of every ten workers were female. A significant number of those workers were children under 15. Grocery, confectionery, fruit and clothing stores, many founded by immigrants and migrants, also served as an important part of Holyoke's economy. As each group of immigrants and migrants arrived – Irish, French Canadians, Italians, Germans, Poles and Puerto Ricans – they adjusted to a new city and joined the competition for jobs, fair wages and conditions, and a better life.

Workers building the dam and canals often performed dangerous tasks. Photograph courtesy of the Wistariahurst Museum Archives.

Irish laborers provided the first immigrant work force in Holyoke, having arrived in 1847 to construct the new dam and mill buildings. When the cotton mills became operative, many of the laborers and their families remained to work because the factory produced coarse goods for which highly trained help was not essential. Of the several hundred first employed in the mills, at least half were Irish, while the remainder were recruited from within Ireland Parish and surrounding towns.

Log drivers used the Connecticut River as a highway. Four hundred men were employed by logging companies around Holyoke. In 1871, Joseph Curtis Lewis constructed a lumber mill above the dam.

The Connecticut railroad shipped finished lumber both east and south on the river. It was the encroachment of the railroad that put logging out of business. The depletion of the old growth forests near the Connecticut River, as well as the rising costs of the lumber company were other reasons logging businesses declined. The last drive of the Connecticut Valley Lumber Company was in 1915.

Holyoke's industries required large machinery to run the mills. For example, Holyoke Machine Company's shop, established in 1863 and built at 517 Main Street, made gears, machinery and water wheels for Holyoke businesses. As the business grew steadily, they began exporting. Finishing machines made at the machine company were shipped to Germany, France and Scotland. Deane Sump Pump Company began

Dam laborers were mostly Irish. Photograph courtesy of the Wistariahurst Museum Archives.

Log drives, especially this one at Log Pond Cove, served an important industry in early Holyoke. Most of the wooden houses in Holyoke were framed with this material. Photograph courtesy of Wistariahurst Museum Archives.

as a rented shop out of the Holyoke Machine Company. George Deane, inventor of the steam pump, commanded a wide market in Holyoke and across the country. However, after years of Holyoke's dependence on Deane's machines, International Pump Company reorganized and George Deane lost control of

Holyoke Machine Company, pictured here in 1883, manufactured large parts that made Holyoke's mills churn. Photograph courtesy of the Wistariahurst Museum Archives.

Many workers, like these in the Holyoke Machine Company, provided much needed supplies for the mills. Photograph courtesy of the Holyoke Public Library History Room.

the local plant he founded. Other companies provided needed goods and services to mills, companies and other businesses in Holyoke. These included the Henry Seymour Cutlery Company, organized in 1839, the Prentiss Wire Mills, established in 1857 and the Massachusetts Screw Company, organized in 1864.

Prentiss Wire Mills. Photograph courtesy of the Wistariahurst Museum Archives.

Early mill workers. Photograph courtesy of the Wistariahurst Museum Archives.

Workers in the mills were on the job at 5:00 AM. At 6:00 am they could stop for an hour long breakfast. Dinner came at 12:15 PM for 45 minutes. At 6:30 PM, workers got another 45 minutes for supper. They often worked until 9:00 PM six days a week. There were no legal regulations of hours or conditions of labor in Massachusetts before 1874. It was considered a person's privilege to work as many hours as they chose, or they were free to starve if they refused to work long hours. A state law of 1867 stipulated that all children under 15 years of age, no matter what background, must be sent to school at least three months out of every year under penalty of fine, to be collected from the employer. However, a survey conducted in 1869 revealed general disregard of that law by most mill owners. In the 151 Massachusetts mill towns where child labor was used, between 5,000 and 6,000 children under the age of 15 were

A child is instructed by her overseer in this textile mill in Holyoke. Photograph taken by Lewis Hine. Photograph courtesy of the Library of Congress, Prints & Photographs Division, National Child Labor Committee Collection.

employed in mills and shops, of whom 60% could not read or write. These early labor regulations governing child labor were critical in shaping the textile industry more than the paper industry because of the paper industry's predominate use of adult male labor. In 1877, 24% of the Holyoke textile mill employees under 20 years of age were illiterate while 15% in the paper mils were illiterate.

Whether an adult or child, work in the mills was hard. Workers did what they had to in order to better their working class lives. Rose Degan, a French Canadian, remembers "my mother giving me a bit of brandy to keep my stomach warm while I walked in the winter [to work]."

Time Table of the Holyoke Mills,

To take effect on and after Jan. 3d, 1853.

The standard being that of the Western Rail Road, which is the Meridian time at Cambridge.

MORNING BELLS.

First Bell ring at 4.40, A. M.   Second Bell ring in at 5, A. M.

YARD GATES

Will be opened at ringing of Morning Bells, of Meal Bells, and of Evening Bells, and kept open ten minutes.

WORK COMMENCES

At ten minutes after last Morning Bell, and ten minutes after Bell which "rings in" from Meals.

BREAKFAST BELLS.

October 1st, to March 31st, inclusive, ring out at 7, A. M.; ring in at 7.30, A. M. April 1st, to Sept. 30th, inclusive, ring out at 6.30, A. M.; ring in at 7, A. M.

DINNER BELLS.

Ring out at 12.30, P. M.; ring in at 1, P. M.

EVENING BELLS.

Ring out at 6.30,* P. M.

* Excepting on Saturdays when the Sun sets previous to 6.30.   At such times, ring out at Sunset.

In all cases, the *first* stroke of the Bell is considered as marking the time.

Early mill bell schedule in 1853. Photograph courtesy of the Wistariahurst Museum Archives.

THE PAPER INDUSTRY

There were many mills producing paper in Holyoke beginning in the early 1850s. Hundreds of thousands of workers were in and out of those mills in a 165 year span. These men, women and children, experienced something that many Americans today cannot say they have experienced – mill work. Paper making was largely considered a man's job because it required heavy lifting and large machinery. In general, female employees were rag sorters or cutters in the paper mills. There was little employment of minors in paper plants but young girls between 16 and 20 had the most desirable jobs in the finishing rooms. In 1880, the Irish formed 38% of the paper work force. Barely 10% of paper workers were French Canadian, who held a higher proportion of the lower-paid jobs in the textile mills.

These men and boys enjoy a swim on the third level canal. National Blank Book is in the background. Photograph courtesy of the Wistariahurst Museum Archives.

Parson's Paper Company, the earliest paper company in Holyoke, started production in 1853. Joseph Parsons, Colonel Aaron Bagg and Whiting Street were the company's founders. Though originally, they had difficulty convincing the Hadley Falls company, which was determined that Holyoke would be a textile city, to rent them a mill site. After they negotiated, the land and power were made available to Parson's Paper. By 1856, they were ready to expand and build a second mill, which would double their capacity for production. The first floor contained engines and Fourdrinier machines, and the second floor was used to store produce and hold rag rooms. They produced fine writing paper, white and tinted envelope paper, and cardboard. Average piece-work earnings of a woman in a paper mill were about $36 a month and the wages by time amounted to between $27 and $29.25 a month; men on a time basis netted from $39 - $91 a month. Though these wages seem small, they were princely compared to the pay in the cotton mills.

National Blank Book, a producer of paper and binder products, was established in 1843. They were a large employer in Holyoke through 1969. Throughout their history, they continued to keep up to date with the newest technologies from producing computer printout binders and storage modules to micrographic supplies, cataloguing systems, and notebooks. In 1967, the company merged with Dennison Manufacturing Company of Framingham, Massachusetts.

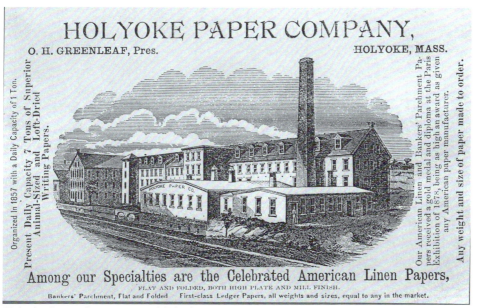

Holyoke Paper Company, established in 1857. Photograph courtesy of the Holyoke Public Library History Room.

In 1857, the former foreman of Parson's Paper Company, D.M. Butterfield, launched a new mill company called Holyoke Paper Company. Among its specialties were flat and folded linen papers, and baker's parchment ruled paper. Average piece work earnings of women in a paper mill in 1867 were about $36 a month.

Whiting Paper Company, established in 1865, created higher grades of paper, wedding paper and Bristol, bond, ledger, linen and extra superfine writing papers. Whiting's rag room employed 110 on one floor. The attic and third floor were for drying paper. The first floor contained two 1,500 pound washers, four 1,200 pound engines, and two rotary bleach boilers of 5,000 pound capacity.

Valley Paper Company, located on the second level canal, was established in 1866. The company produced fine writing and envelope paper at a capacity of 2.5 tons a day. The Riverside Paper Company, organized that same year, made fine writing paper at capacity of 3 tons per day. Beginning its manufacturing of fine book, writing and envelope paper in white, tinted or color finish, the Franklin Paper Company had sixty presses and worked at a capacity of 3 tons per day.

The 1870s was a year of growth for paper manufacturers in Holyoke. Union Paper Manufacturing, organized in 1870 by Henry and Edwin Dickinson and J.E. Taylor, purchased property of Bemis Paper Company, and manufactured fine writing and collar

Riverside Paper Company, c. late 1880s. Photograph courtesy of the Holyoke Public Library History Room.

Whiting Paper Company, located on the first canal, was one of the few companies that did not merge to form the American Writing Paper Company. Pictured late 1800s. Photograph courtesy of the Holyoke Public Library History Room.

Holyoke Envelope Company employees outside the office at South Main Street, c. 1890s. Photograph courtesy of the Wistariahurst Museum Archives.

paper. Crocker Manufacturing Company, mill No. 1 was erected in 1870 and was intended for the manufacture of collar paper only. The company later purchased the old Albion Mill, named Crocker Manufacturing Company, mill No. 2. The Beebe and Holbrook Paper Company, makers of fine writing paper, was built in 1871 by the Hampden Paper Company. Their product consisted largely of the finest grades of white and tinted wedding folios and linen papers, also lines of flat and ruled writing papers at 2.5 tons per day. The Excelsior Mill, established on the third level canal in 1872, contained rag cutters, dusters, and rag rooms. They manufactured book and press paper at a capacity of two tons per day. The Newton Paper Company, built in fall of 1873, manufactured corrugated carpet lining, building paper, straw boards, and manila wrapping papers. Holyoke Manilla Mill, organized in 1875 by Mr. Robinson and Mr. Black, produced 2,500 pounds a day. The Albion Paper Company, built by D.H. and J.C. Newton, completed in 1878 with two brick buildings was able to produce two tons per day. J.W. Arnold and Company, organized in 1878, manufactured 1.5 tons of manila paper a day. The Wauregan Paper Mill, owned by James H. Newton, was built in 1879. It had a capacity of producing 5 tons of fine book, envelope and writing paper, white and tinted a day. The Nonotuck Paper Company was organized in 1880 by J.S. McElwain.

Massasoit Paper Manufacturing Company, made several brands of choice linen papers, like "crown Leghorn," "imperial parchment", and "Lyons parchment, silk finish." Hadley Falls Paper Company was an offshoot of the Carew Manufacturing Company, located at Hadley Falls.

The Chemical Paper Company, producing new book and writing

Chemical Paper Company, located on the third level canal, 1887. Photograph courtesy of the Wistariahurst Museum Archives.

paper, was owned by the four Newton brothers and was the largest paper mill when it was built in 1880. Though originally founded as the Newton Company with Moses and James Newton in 1876, it eventually was jointly established by the four brothers, John and Daniel, into the Chemical Paper Company. In 1913, Clifton Crocker and Frank McElwain purchased the old Chemical Paper plant and created a more efficient company.

In 1899, a merger occurred when consolidation was needed in the paper companies. American Writing Paper Company, incorporated in New Jersey, comprised 25 mills, 16 of them in Holyoke. These were Albion Paper Company, Beebe & Holbrook, Connecticut River Paper Company, Crocker Manufacturing, George R. Dickinson Paper, Esleek Paper Company, George C. Gill Paper, Holyoke Paper Company, Linden Paper Company, Massasoit Paper Company, Mt. Tom Paper Company, Nonotuck Paper (two mills), Normen Paper, Parsons Paper (one mill), Riverside Paper (two mills), and Wauregan Paper Company.

American Pad & Paper Company (AMPAD) was founded in 1888 by Thomas W. Holley, a young employee

The Newton Brothers are pictured here, c. 1890s, from left to right and top to bottom: Solan, Joseph, Moses, Daniel, John and James. Photograph courtesy of the Wistariahurst Museum Archives

of a local paper mill. Holley noted that ruled pads and paper were not being produced in Holyoke. He used a source of paper called "sortings" and from that he was able to build a great product. AMPAD was built modestly in one room on Main and Dwight Streets. In 1894, a new building at the corner of Winter and Appleton Streets was built to expand. The building was renovated in 1909, doubling its facility. In 2004, AMPAD, like many large companies in America, moved its operations to Mexico, where it is cheaper to find labor.

The land around Holyoke was largely cleared of tress for use in agriculture, and the regrowth after the abandonment of agriculture resulted in young forests, not useful for harvesting paper pulp. The paper industry dwindled because of a shift in the market toward pulp paper, which was of little supply in Holyoke.

American Pad and Paper Company's vacant building on Winter and Appleton Streets, 2006.

THE TEXTILE INDUSTRY

French Canadians were predominantly operatives in the textile mills, and the number of women and children exceeded the number of men. At all skill levels, French Canadians made up 43% of the textile workers while only 17% were Irish. The Census of 1890 indicated that 58% of the French Canadian immigrants were employed in manufacturing or mechanical industries. 18% were in domestics, agriculture, 13% in fishing and mining, 9% in trade and transportation and 1% in professional occupations. The number of female employees in all of these industries was high. French Canadian parents put their children to work as soon as possible and kept them there to evade the state school laws. The adult wage average was cut by the number of children employed. Children were paid from 37 - 80 cents a day. For example, the Lyman Mills, employing only 53 minors out of a total 1,100 persons in 1871, reported its average wage per employee to be 54 cents daily or $163.63 a year. In the thread mills, women rated from 75 cents to $1.60 a day and men from $1 to $2.25 a day. ($1 in 1890 equalled about $20 in 2000 in terms of buying power.) The woolen mills generally paid by piece work but the average daily wage in 1871 was listed at $1.52. In 1880, half of Holyoke's work force (3600) labored in textile mills. 60% of the workers were women and a significant number of those were children under 15. Large mills like Farr Alpaca and Lyman Mills produced thousands of yards of textiles a year. Other smaller companies like Buttrick and Flanders, manufacturers of spindles, bolsters and steps, and Conner Brothers, manufactures of wool extracts, shoddy and flocks, produced smaller quantities of product than most of the larger mills.

Anna Sullivan, longtime resident of Holyoke and union organizer remembers that her mother "did not like the idea of me going into a mill. But that was the only thing you could get into. You see, Holyoke, Chicopee, all our areas, Easthampton, were all large textile sanctuaries and this was all you really had to do, outside of the paper mills and most of them employed just men, very few women worked in the paper mills. And about the only thing you could get into was the textile mills. We had thousands of workers in Holyoke alone in the textile mills."

Textile mills began early but faded into Holyoke's history in the 1950s and 1960s. There were a few textile mills that lasted for decades. Hadley Company Spool Cotton Manufactory was built by Hadley Falls Company and used as a machine shop in 1848 until the company began to use it for thread making. Before its existence as a cotton thread mill in 1859, the machine shop made turbine wheels, conduit pipes of iron, gasometers and castings. The Lyman Mills Corporation organized in 1854, producing standard sheeting, flannels and drills. The mill held approximately 1,556 looms in the mills' three buildings. In 1871, 402 males, and 800 females worked there.

A labor shortage in the spring of 1859 led to the first importation of French Canadians to Holyoke. An agent of the Lyman Mills, Mr. Proulx made arrangements to recruit French Canadians and persuade them

Lyman Mill agent in 1883 in front of the Lyman Cotton Mills. Photograph courtesy of the Wistariahurst Museum Archives.

to work and live in Holyoke. In his wagon specially built for carrying passengers, Proulx went from village to village in Quebec and spoke of the prospect of money wages which could be sent home or brought back. He was instructed to secure skilled workers if he could find them, but there were none. Proulx received $4 or $5 for each of 45 girls and 6 men he brought back to Holyoke. Though cotton mill work was hard, young women were preferred over men because of their greater dexterity.

The picker house in a cotton mill was a process that required strong men who could weigh a bale of cotton, the first step in the process of cloth production. After weighing the bales, the pickers opened and mixed the contents into a large bin to form a "bing", which homogenized the raw cotton and filters out the dirt.

The picker then took the fleece and put it through a blower, producing a long smooth sheet or "lap", ready to be wound on wooden drums and delivered to the carding engine. Although most Holyoke picker rooms were clean and well-ventilated, this was hot and dirty work, as the operation of the picker filled the air with flying dust. Anna Sullivan remembered working in the cotton mills: "I don't think many kids went for this work. You came out

The Lyman Mills are currently at the site of Open Square. Photograph courtesy of the Holyoke Public Library History Room.

looking like Santa Claus. Your hair was covered with cotton, your clothes with cotton, you ate cotton. It was, ... all cotton."

Recruiting was a normal way to attract immigrants to certain jobs, especially when agents could travel over the Canadian border. At the Lyman Mills, paymaster Stephen Holman maintained regular correspondence with a number of banks, travel agencies and former employees in England and Scotland who sent workers his way. The recruiters assured Holman that women whom they recommended were both competent and of good character. Holman's reputation for paternalism was so strong that one Scottish woman wrote him inquiring whether he knew anything about her daughter, who had not communicated with her in more than a year.

In 1862 the Lyman Mills raw cotton supply ran out because of the Civil War and they had to close the mill. Out of a population of about 4,600 French Canadian, 700 were thrown out of work. The following year, the city received a boost because of the demand for uniforms for the Union Army. Woolen and silk mills began to appear along with businesses that supplied these factories, creating a spirit of hustle and bustle of industrial Holyoke. For example, Beebe, Webber and Company's Woolen Mills, established in 1863, produced 450,000 yards of wool per year. Jared Beebe reported in 1870 that there were 33 young persons

This woman winds at the Merrick Thread Mills. Photograph courtesy of the Holyoke Public Library History Room.

under the age of 15 years employed in his woolen mill, all of whom worked 69 hours a week. This was despite the law that required children to go to school. The New York Woolen Mill, built in 1864, produced 360,000 yards of wool cloth per year.

By the Civil War, demand for machine made, standardized goods was increasing. Machine tools, agricultural and mining machinery, locomotives, turbines and other machines for paper and cotton mills opened up opportunities for other lines of work in Holyoke. In post-Civil War Holyoke, some manufacturers embraced to the idea that individual labor was the source of wealth, and hard work and self improvement would bring material success to anyone willing to make the effort. It is in this concept that more mills were formed in the 1870s.

Timothy and John Merrick built the Merrick Thread Company in 1865. A year later, it became American Thread Company, located on Canal Street. Merrick Thread Company originated in 1865, as an outgrowth of a partnership with Timothy Merrick, Austin Merrick and Origen Hall, and was located in Mansfield Connecticut. It moved to Holyoke in 1865 due to its huge success and growth. It was an example of a mill that was run with absentee ownership. After the Merricks built the company in 1866, and added to its equipment in 1871, there were over three hundred employees there. Thus, Timothy moved to Holyoke and watched over the business. By 1887, they were making 48 million spools of cotton thread each year. However, after Timothy Merrick died the company became the American Thread Company, located on Canal Street. In general, business expanded in 1916 and the capacity of the mill was enlarged and 2000

These employees pose for a photograph behind American Thread Mills in c. 1920s. Photograph courtesy of the Wistariahurst Museum Archives.

American Thread Mills thread winder c. 1915. Photograph courtesy of the Wistariahurst Museum Archives.

employees were given a 5% wage increase. When business decreased after World War I, wages were cut.

Mabelle Martin Bowen remembered her father working in the dressing room at the Merrick Thread Mills: "The temperature was so high in that room that the men wore hardly any clothes during their work hours. And they'd have to stop work at a certain hour — maybe 9 o'clock in the morning. And that was to sort of revive them. They were so perspired out."

The Germania Mills were located on the third level of the canal system, pictured here in the late 1880s. Photograph courtesy of the Wistariahurst Museum Archives.

It was around the 1860s to 1880s when Germany began furnishing Holyoke with a steady, though not large, group of workers. The Germania Mills, located on the first canal system, was started in 1865 by two German brothers, Hermann and August Stursberg, who were Rhineland manufacturers. Highly skilled spinners and weavers had traveled with the Stursbergs from Germany. Spinners and weavers were brought from Germany to work in the mills. The German community was smaller than the British community, which in 1880 was 5% of Holyoke's population, comprising a little more than 2% of the population. A German colony grew up around the mills in South Holyoke.

Kathryn Werner Dietel of South Hadley Falls, Massachusetts worked at the Germania Mills in the 1890s. Kathryn was the first loom worker at Germania Mills. She was originally from Stammbach Franconia Bavaria Germany and worked in the textile mills there. She married Charles J. Dietel, who worked as a bookbinder at National Blank Book. They later ran a bakery on Bardwell Street in South Hadley Falls. Their eldest son, Charles Jr., ran Dietel Drug Store for many years.

In the 1920s, the spinning department at the Farr Alpaca Mills on Jackson Street in Holyoke employed Stella Baran and Julia Werbiskis Gardner as doffers. At the Farr Alpaca dye house women were paid $12-14 a week. Photograph courtesy of the Wistariahurst Museum Archives.

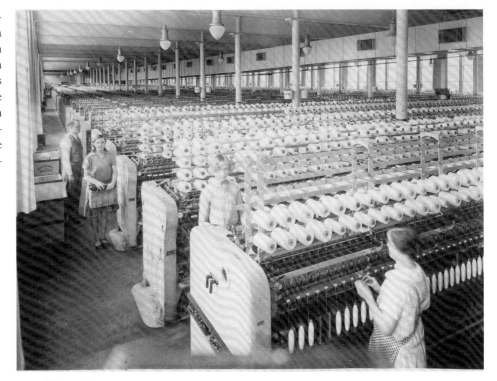

Mary Allen Barnes works at Farr Alpaca in 1915. Photograph courtesy of the Holyoke Public Library History Room.

Another textile company, the Farr Alpaca Company, was established to produce woolen goods in 1873, the same year Holyoke was incorporated as a city. Machinery was brought down from Canada in 1874. Over half the employees were from Canada or England, where they were trained in the specialties of handling long fibers of alpaca wool. From the beginning, their quality textiles made the company famous. For instance, they were awarded the first prize in competition with exhibitors from all over the world at the Centennial Exposition in the first two years of their operations.

Farr Alpaca constantly added to its mills and the number and quality of its products. In 1923, the mill completed a 75,000 spindle cotton plant, which was two to three times the size of the new cotton mill and replaced its outmoded power plant at tremendous cost. 750 different kinds of cloth were produced using 150 different processes for making textiles.

Both the Lyman Mills and the Farr Alpaca Company showed a marked increase in Polish workers during the 1890s. The mills worked 66 hours a week and paid workers weekly wages of $4.20 on Saturday afternoon. This influx of people increased the supply of labor and kept wages low. Together with a number of Russian Jews, the Poles comprised about 15% of the city's residents by 1910 as compared to less than 1% in 1885. Poles who loved to farm, worked just long enough in the mills to save enough money and buy their own land. Many of the Polish people who are successful were farmers in Hadley, Whately, Amherst and Granby, got their start in Holyoke mills.

Working conditions at Farr Alpaca were hot and loud. Many workers would use hand signals to communicate when machines were running. Desire DeVries, second generation French Canadian, said, "My sisters and my mother worked in the Alpaca. In fact, I was fourteen years old and my sister got me a job in the Alpaca because at 14 you had to go to work. I got $3.20 a week. And it was so hot and you couldn't open the window and I went home for dinner and I forgot to come back."

The Farr Alpaca Company was committed to the welfare of its employees. The company provided a recreational auditorium for its 4,000 workers that was the center of activities. There were dramatic productions, music and dances, sponsored and organized by the employees themselves. There was an athletic field and a dispensary with a physician and a dentist.

Skinner & Sons Silk Manufacturing Company, originally established in Haydenville in 1839, moved to Holyoke in 1874 after the dam burst, causing the Mill River to flood and destroy the factory. The company built its success with silk thread but then went on to create products like satin sleeve linings, silk serges, silk and mohair braids, button hole twist, sewings, organizine and cashmere sewings, eventually producing over 7,000 pounds a month. The Skinner silk manufacturing business grew to have sales of $6.5 million in 1902 with 2,500 employees.

Eugenie Cote was born in France in 1904. Her parents immigrated to Holyoke when she was seven years old. When she was fourteen, she went to work for the Skinner Mills and worked there from 1918 to 1940. She said, "There were always quite a few openings [for jobs]…There was one time that work must have been slow or something because the ones that had their husbands working, they got laid off for a while but ..... I worked steady."

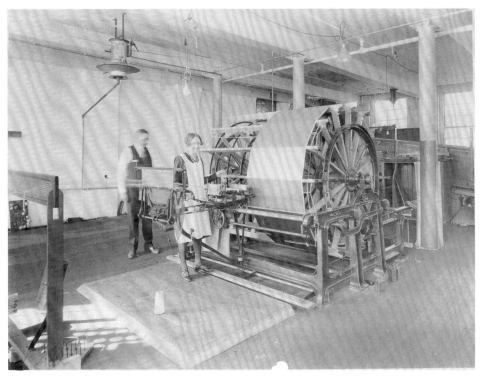

Eugenie Cote stands at the warping machine at the William Skinner & Sons Silk Manufacturing Company in 1926. Photograph courtesy of the Wistariahurst Museum Archives.

In 1909, sixty young women were employed at Skinner Silks at $4 a week to spend a few hours of each day to learn the exacting art of silk weaving. The mill management did this to create a trained reserve corps of help. An anonymous employee at Skinners described her supervisor Gus Dubrois as "stern, he wanted the work done good….you had to dress up to work for Dubrois. Yes Sir. You had to be clean and you had to be well-dressed in there. Because the job we did, you'd never dirty your hands even. We'd sit on a chair and we'd pull the silk in front of us. And the floors in the factory were so immaculate. Not like today. It was clean, very clean."

Over the 87 years of operation in Holyoke, the Skinner Silk Manufacturing company produced an array of fabrics from their earliest origins of silk, cotton backed satin, and pure dye taffetas, to washable crepes, rayon, and Tackle Twill. The mills produced silk for parachutes as part of the war effort in the 1940s. In 1944, the company began producing synthetics like nylon as there was a shift in the general market. Most popular among the later lines of Skinner materials was their bridal satin, remembered today by many brides of the 1940s and 1950s. In 1961, the Skinner family sold the business, with all of their trademarks and

Desire DeVries is the third from the front on the right in the weaving room at the Bond Street plant of Skinner Silk Manufacturing, 1928. Photograph courtesy of the Wistariahurst Museum Archives.

patents, to Indian Head Mills, who closed the mills a year later. The mill buildings were destroyed in a fire in 1980. Holyoke Heritage State Park was built on that site.

Mr. Desire DeVries said in 1989, "I was a cotton boy in Skinners. You had to do odds and ends, like that. If you had to go to the other mills, across the street on Appleton Street to get some silk for the spinners and whatever supplies that the loom fixers needed, I had to get it for them."

Joseph Hampson founded a textile factory at 58 Canal Street. In 1938 he deeded the property to his son, Walter Hampson, and Walter named the business the Clinton Silk Mill. The Clinton Silk Mill was named after Walter Hampson's first born son, Clinton W. Hampson. Their silk was used in the production of

Above: Gus Dubrois is the foreman in the center of the photo of these female inspecting workers in 1926 at the Skinner Silk Manufacturers. Below: The weavers of Skinners in 1928. DeVries is fifth from the left in the front row. Photographs courtesy of the Wistariahurst Museum Archives.

Inside of the Clinton Silk Mills, c. 1950s. W. Roy Hampson is on the right and Clinton W. Hampson is on the left. Photograph courtesy of the Hampson Family.

parachutes during World War II. The mill also wove cotton and synthetic cloth. The synthetic cloth was used for lining in suit coats. Two of Walter Hampson's sons took over the running of the company approximately in 1951. Clinton W. Hampson was the President and W. Roy Hampson was the Vice President. The brothers remained in the business until 1970 when W. Roy Hampson left the family business. Clinton W. Hampson ran the business until 1976, when he sold the property to Hadley Printing Company. Thirty years later, Hadley Printing remains at this site today.

Some mills, like Skinner's Silk, changed their product with changing times. When after 1940, a large infusion of military contracts, promising unprecedented profits, stabilized the regional industry and led some manufacturers to reopen deserted plants. The Lyman and Farr Alpaca mill closings indicated the decline of the New England textile industry was beginning. Between 1920 and 1940, Massachusetts lost nearly 45% of its textile production jobs. Power sources, like electricity, were more efficient than the water power being used. During this period nearly 200 mills were shut down. Others reduced their scale of operations. The decline of the New England textile industry had lasting consequences, not simply for the local communities but for the entire region and the rest of the country as well. Competition for remaining jobs increased due to many layoffs.

Photograph of a faded sign of Armour Provisions downtown Holyoke, 2006. Armour and Company, wholesale meat and provision sellers, was established in 1906 at 46 Race Street. In 1923 it moved to 130 Race Street, then later moved to 24 Race Street, where it stayed until 1943.

THE LABOR MOVEMENT IN HOLYOKE

All immigrant groups shared the problem of low wages, long hours and poor working conditions. Irish wage earners viewed increased immigration from French Canadians during the late 19th century with genuine alarm, believing the influx would destabilize regional labor markets and undermine existing work and wage standards. At this point, Irish workers began encountering "No Irish Need Apply" signs in the mills. French Canadian immigrants were willing to work more hours for less pay. However, it has been said that the French Canadian practice of sending kids to work in the mills early coupled with their reluctance to participate in strikes and join unions, added to the fears that gave rise to ethnic stereotypes that branded Franco Americans as congenital scabs. These caricatures soon appeared in the studies of state labor agencies and other media. French Canadian community leaders protested these stereotypes, but in doing so, they admitted the tendency of French Canadian immigrants to avoid strikes as it was not reverent to law and order.

In 1876 a mass meeting of unemployed workers marched upon City Hall to demand that the Board of Aldermen build a new sewer to supply work. "We did not come to this country to starve," cried one person, recorded by a reporter of the Transcript in September 16, 1876. In the fall of 1878 women who had supported families on their earnings as rag sorters in the fine writing paper mills asked the city for help when their hours were cut. The Socialist Labor Party, Knights of Labor, and Trades and Labor Assembly institutionally represented the Holyoke working class, but their membership included only a part of the local working class. German workers joined all three groups, but only the more skilled Irish workers participated, and French Canadians were not represented.

In the early industrial days of Holyoke, there was little resistance among textile workers in the mills because of paternalism among some of the mill owners of Skinners, Farr Alpaca and Lyman Mills. As a result, the workers also placed a great importance on the relationship between overseers and workers. The key to effective functioning of this textile paternalism was the overseer and the textile workers understood the overseer's role. The overseer hired workers and ruled on petitions for better working conditions, transfers and pay increases. Local newspapers would often run notices of workers giving their foreman gifts. Mill paternalism was successful in diffusing malcontent of the first generation of industrial workers from Ireland and Canada. Paternalism even worked into the late 1870s as a large wave of French Canadians entered the mills and were as submissive as their predecessors.

Additionally, ethnic conflict among Irish, French-Canadian, and Polish workers hindered efforts at organizing the textile industry. The massive influx of French Canadians in the late 1870s threatened textile operatives. There were stories floating around that some French Canadians offered to work for only 25 cents a day, and because they sent their children to work in the mills instead of to school, many textile workers feared losing their jobs. The Irish felt particularly threatened because they were the workers least likely to possess skills. In response to the threat, fights begun in textile mills carried over into the city streets.

Craft exclusiveness separated skilled from unskilled workers. Less skilled workers in the rag and finishing departments had little success with their sporadic job actions in gaining higher wages. Managers paid little attention to their grievances because they were easily replaced. In textiles, shop floor kin networks served as an

Fraternal Order of the Eagles Lodge parade down Main Street in the 1920s. Photograph courtesy of the Holyoke Public Library History Room.

important substitute for trade unions. Particularly among the French-Canadians kin networks placed and assisted newcomers, protected group members from mistreatment, and generally eased one through the day. Not until the organizing drives of the 1930s, boosted by the legal protection of the National Labor Relations Act and other New Deal measures, would Holyoke's paper and textile unions achieve real stability and city-wide recognition.

As the dominant ethnic group in Holyoke at the beginning of the 1840s, the Irish workers had a history of labor protest going back to 1848 when Irish workers building the canals struck over a wage reduction. The Irish were not only involved in the Knights of Labor, but were heavily involved with the Democratic Party. Some Irish in Holyoke, like the Lynch brothers, the Connors brother, and the O'Connell family, moved successfully into the employer class.

The paper industry had always worked longer hours than any other. Two shifts of workmen had sufficed to keep machines in operation from midnight Sunday to midnight Saturday. In some mills, a paper maker worked 11 hours a day in alternate weeks or 13 hours a night. The Eagle Lodge, the first paper maker's union in the country, campaigned in the mid 1880s to gain Saturday evening or Monday mornings off without losing pay. They presented the case to a Convention of American Paper Manufacturers in 1886 and 1887. From this, the Newton Paper Company inaugurated a shorter week on the theory that the care of workers was essential to success in paper manufacturing, rather than the long hours and low wages. Successful paper companies also had an intelligent and loyal workforce, a fact that distinguished Holyoke as the Paper City. William Whiting took the lead among writing paper manufacturers and agreed to a 60 hour week instead of a 72 hour week. However, the Convention failed to put the agreement into practice throughout the industry, so their agreements fell through.

Of the three dominant ethnic groups in Holyoke, Germans were the smallest in the workforce, but they were the most highly organized. They were more predisposed than the Irish or French Canadians to labor organization, and a small but active group was involved in the Socialist Labor Party. In the 1880s, the party brought Socialists such as Johann Most, Karl Marx's daughter Eleanor and her husband Edward Aveling, and the German Socialist leader Wilhelm Liebknect to speak to the working people of Holyoke. On February 4, 1886, nearly 100 German weavers walked out at Skinner Silk Mill, demanding weekly pay, reinstatement of a fired co-worker, and the dismissal of David Goetz, an abusive overseer, who was allegedly partial in distributing work. At first, William Skinner refused to admit that his workers had any real grievances and blamed the strike on "the employees of another mill, who are connected with the socialists." Skinner realized that he was mistaken and two weeks later sat down with arbitrator C.H. Litchman, affiliated with the Knights of Labor, to try to reach a settlement. Sixteen days later Litchman announced that with the exception of discharging Goetz, Skinner met most of the grievances. But because Skinner refused to rehire 15 strikers whom he thought organized the strike, the strike continued. The strikers received active support from the national Socialist Labor Party and the Knights of Labor. The Socialist Labor Party contacted the New York City Central Labor Union and secured assurances that 17 organizations representing 4000 tailors would boycott Skinner products. Skinner won out after strikers tried to accuse Goetz of being a Mormon. Goetz was not let go, but the strikers were rehired.

The first Holyoke local assembly of the Knights of Labor was organized in November 1882 with 14 members. The activities of the Holyoke Knights were directed toward the passage of a weekly payments law, shortening the hours of the paper mill workers and strike arbitration. The Knights of Labor got involved in the paper mill workers' campaign to shorten their weekend hours. Hours of labor were much on the minds of workers in post-Civil War Massachusetts. A law passed in 1874 had restricted to 60 hours per week for women and children employed in manufacturing corporations. This effectively shortened the workday for all textile mill employees, but the paper mills, which employed far fewer women and children and in less strategic jobs in the overall manufacturing operation, were hardly affected.

On a national scale, labor unions organized a strike in 1886 for an eight hour work day in Chicago. The Knights of Labor led 80,000 people down a main street in downtown Chicago, and within a few days, they were joined nationwide by 350,000 more workers. A fight broke out near the picket lines and police had to intervene. Fliers were distributed and called for a rally at Haymarket Square, a commercial center downtown Chicago. The fliers inflamed the prior incident and suggested that police had murdered the strikers on behalf of business interests. The rally took place quite peacefully, with many witnesses and even the mayor had stopped by to watch. On duty police officers ordered the rally to disperse and a bomb was thrown at the police line, killing one. The police immediately retaliated by firing into the crowd. A total of 11 people died.

After the Haymarket Square rally in Chicago, some anti-German sentiment spread across the nation, even to Holyoke. This stemmed from the feeling that labor dissatisfaction was a result of social anarchist German agitators. A working man wrote the Transcript newspaper in late 1886 in favor of weekly payments signed his letter "Not a Rosenberg."

In 1893, the organization of the International Brotherhood of Paper Makers - with a national charter from the American Federation of Labor - formed as a result of the Eagle Lodge's failure to launch the aforementioned agreement at the Convention. The workers' issues were no longer on a local scale. A successful strike in 1901 in the paper mills guaranteed machine tenders 66 hours per week. However, it would take another 15 years for organized labor in the papermaking industry to become a powerful force.

1891 Central Labor Union Field Day Ribbon. In Holyoke, the union coordinated local activity, counting 17 member locals representing 1,600 workers by 1892. From the collection of Wistariahurst Museum.

CONSTITUTION

OF THE

INTERNATIONAL

LADIES' GARMENT WORKERS' UNION

AND

BY-LAWS

FOR LOCAL UNIONS

1917

NEW YORK

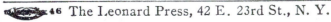

46 The Leonard Press, 42 E. 23rd St., N. Y.

A page from the small book containing bylaws for local unions. Miss Angelina Moggs received this booklet when she was initiated on November 23, 1917. She paid an initiation fee of $5.45. From the collection of Wistariahurst Museum.

In May of 1898, 400 weavers walked out at Farr Alpaca Company, demanding a 10% wage increase and abolition of fines for production of poor cloth. Because business had just returned to pre-depression levels, Farr wished to avoid an extended struggle. In 1899, the strikers at Farr Alpaca, mostly French Canadian women, accepted a company offer to revise the fine system and increase wages by 5%, but not before they had formed a union. Within a few weeks, the Polish and French Canadian weavers at Lyman Mills also established separate unions and joined operatives in other departments in seeking to restore the more favorable 1896 wage schedule.

Only German operatives at the Germania Woolen Mills mounted serious resistance. The Germania Mills slashed wages 20% after a three week shutdown in February 1894, which was the second cut in two months; 200

When the workers were on strike, the machines were silent at Farr Alpaca. Photograph courtesy of the Wistariahurst Museum Archives.

operatives walked out. Eventually, they came to terms with a decrease in return for a 10% increase in rent of the company's tenements. Winter 1876 brought the formation of a German speaking chapter of the Workingmen's Party (the Socialist Labor Party in America) in Holyoke. Limited largely to Germans, the Socialist Labor Party's base of operations was the Turnverein in Springdale, which became a focal point of socialist culture.

Strikes that occurred nationwide had a huge affect on local industries in Holyoke. For example, the national textile strike that began on September 1, 1934 eventually caused over 3500 people in Holyoke to strike the mills of William Skinner & Sons, Farr Alpaca, American Thread Company, the Clinton Silk Mill, the Jennings Company, the Mabson Silk Company, Livingston Worsted Mills (formerly known as Germania Mills), and D. Mackintosh & Sons. Skinner posted a sign on the bulletin board outside his mills that read, "These mills were open Tuesday for regular operation. Not enough reported for work to warrant keeping open. Therefore, these mills are closed indefinitely. You can receive your last week's pay as usual on our regular pay day, Thursday." Strikers rallied together to hear from the president of the Central Labor Union, the vice-president of the Holyoke Silk and Rayon Workers' Union, and Mary Lizak, who addressed the strikers in Polish. There occurred slight incidents of violence, including one where a group of picketers at the Cabot Street entrance of Farr Alpaca shoved a middle aged woman to her knees. Her lunch was dumped into the street and her coffee spilled over a passerby. A few days into the strike, however, only 15 strikers had applied for welfare aid. By September 20, 1934 over 2,000 people attended a benefit dance for strikers at O'Brien's Gold and Black ballroom. The dance was the first public benefit function sponsored by the strikers and was held to raise money meant to defray costs of the strike. At the event, there were tap dancers, dance duets, and acrobatic waltzes.

Anna Sullivan, born into a family of textile workers, was a leader in organizing the drive of the Amalgamated Textile Workers Union during the 1930s. The union brought the first 40 hour week to Skinner & Sons Manufacturing in 1936. She was hired by the Congress of Industrial Organizations (CIO) in 1938 as a full-time organizer, and she eventually became the vice-president of the Massachusetts CIO. Sullivan remembers how she "organized in Easthampton, Ludlow, door-to-door and leafleting factories. I had three types of leaflets - - in Polish, in French and in English. The people came out and waited to get their leaflet…From that, we built up. We came up a whole lot compared to what we ever had."

One laborer remembered that in the 1940s or so, there was "one strike that involved [Parson's Paper Company]; it was only because we were one of a whole group of paper mills that used to bargain together with the union…we had to close our doors. Our people showed up to go to work but we had to keep them out because we were part of the common negotiating group….the strike lasted about a week at most."

HOLYOKE'S OTHER BUSINESSES

While the workers in the mills had some opportunity to rally for better wages and working conditions, there were many employees of businesses in Holyoke besides mills, for whom that was not an option. These businesses often relied on family members for generations to run a successful business. Many immigrants found a niche in the service industries that provided necessary items for people in town. Markets like the Great Atlantic and Pacific Tea Company provided Holyokers with much needed groceries. Smaller companies like Vollert's Dairy made milk deliveries for years downtown.

The Great Atlantic and Pacific Tea Company was located in the Highlands, pictured here in c. 1900s. Photograph courtesy of the Holyoke Public Library History Room.

Vollert's Dairy workers pictured are Frank Scheinost, Max Vollert, and Richard Giroux. The Vollerts began their company when they used horse and buggy to make deliveries. Photograph courtesy of the Wistariahurst Museum Archives.

Paul Cote's meat market was located on Cabot Street in South Holyoke. Photograph courtesy of the Wistariahurst Museum Archives.

Paul C. Cote, born in Canada, was brought up and educated in Holyoke. His store, located at 146 Cabot Street, was one of the most familiar stores in South Holyoke, and successfully competed with other grocery markets. He sold breakfast goods, fine canned goods, teas, coffees and cake from the Oak Grove Creamery, as well as fresh vegetables, butter and cheese.

Thomas S. Child established his shoe store in 1864, just as Holyoke was becoming an important industrial center in Massachusetts. Every so often there would be an order for a dozen bedroom slippers from a Mrs. Lapointe, also known as Carrie Pratt, who ran the local entertainment house on Lower Westfield Road. When this many slippers were ordered, it was clear that her girls, Bubbles, Irene, Grace, Maud and others, needed new bedroom slippers.

Thomas Child's shoe store, 1899. Photograph courtesy of the Holyoke Public Library History Room.

George Nye Company Wholesale Meats. Photograph courtesy of the Holyoke Public Library History Room.

Vautrian's barbershop on 109 High Street, late 1800s. Photograph courtesy of the Holyoke Public Library History Room.

Elzear Vautrain arrived from Canada in the mid 1870s and worked for Hadley Falls Company where he learned English before starting his barbershop. There was a second hand store in the basement of his High Street Shop. Joseph Rigali, another early immigrant to Holyoke, owned a fruit store next door.

Pierre Bonvouloir, of French Canadian descent, was born at Sainte Brigide in 1854. He began a grocery and provision business in Holyoke in 1875 at 103 High Street. His business flourished for years. He elected to the City Council, the School Committee, and the City Treasurer. He was a member of the Society St. Jean Baptiste, Union Canadiene, Le Chasseurs Club, and the Knights of Columbus. There are many stories of immigrants coming to Holyoke and later starting their own business. Abraham Marx was born in Germany, came to Holyoke in 1877, and settled at 200 Pine Street. He had a tailor shop at 81 Main Street. After 1890, the business moved to High Street and Division.

Duncan MacLean's Pastry Shop opened for business in the early 1950s at 415 High Street. This Scottish immigrant became known for his meat pies. People traveled from as far away as Cape Cod, Boston and Hartford to sample the Scotch delicacy. In 1961, the restaurant moved to 290 High Street.

Christopher Orsini, son of Italian immigrants Andrew Orsini and Clara Equi, was born and raised in Holyoke. Orsini's Luncheonette was built at the Old Flatiron in the Flats in 1889. He later had two stores, which he gave to his sons Chris, Jr., and Andrew. In 1964, however, the sons sold the business to the Schmitter family.

Fred U. Menard, born in Quebec, was the oldest French Canadian grocer and meat cutter in Holyoke. He came to Holyoke in 1865 at the age of 18. His store was located at 40 Cabot Street and offered the highest grades of staple and fancy groceries of all kinds, sold at the lowest possible prices.

Theobald Hegy came to Holyoke after the Franco-Prussian war and worked as a dyer in the New York Woolen Mills, which the Stursburgs later bought and called Germania Mills. Hegy Cleaners Press Room, established by Theobald in 1878, was a factory that cleaned and dyed garments, rugs, carpets, draperies, household furnishings, upholstered furniture and even the interior of closed cars. Services also included insurance on all items in their

Patrick Joseph (P.J.) Sheehan, born in Killorglin, Ireland, immigrated to Holyoke through Charlestown, MA, in 1890. Though he first worked on the Holyoke dam, he later became a teamster then a dairy farmer. The house he bought on the corner of Route 202 and Homestead Avenue eventually became the Sheehan Dairy Farm. Holyoke Community College was built on his former pasture land. When P.J. passed away in 1946, his sons Cornelius, Michael, and John operated the farm. Pictured here are P.J. and his first grandchild, Jack Conway. Photograph courtesy of Angela Conway.

Hegy Cleaners, c. 1920s. Photograph courtesy of the Holyoke Public Library History Room.

possession while cleaning or dyeing. In 1916, the cleaners had so much business that a new building was built in Springdale.

John Heinritz arrived in America in 1851 at 18 years of age from Sparneck, Bavaria. The journey took 57 days and passengers had to cook their own meals. In 1866 he worked as a weaver at Germania Mills. In 1879 he established the drugstore at the corner of Main and Hamilton with his eldest son that specialized in mill chemicals. The store was known for a complete line of over 400 varieties of herbs. Early pharmacists performed vaccinations and eye tests. The store was more than a place where drugs were sold in South Holyoke; at one time, tickets for the Opera House were sold there. In addition, customers could mail letters and purchase hardware, glass, paint and other materials.

Magri Fruit Company, on Lincoln Street in Holyoke, was run by Mario and Lou Magri. Photograph courtesy of the Wistariahurst Museum Archives.

Christopher Equi had a confectionary store on Maple Street in Holyoke. Photograph courtesy of the Holyoke Public Library History Room.

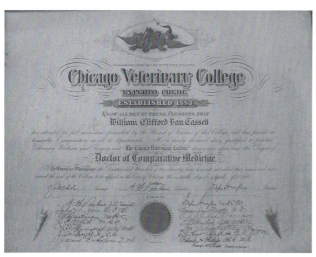

Dr. William VanTassel was a migrant from the midwest. He studied at Chicago's Veterinary College and in 1909 was offered a contract to set up an office in Holyoke. He was contracted to care for the City's horses. From the collection of The Wagner Family.

Hampden Brewing Company, c. 1950s. Hampden Brewing Company had an old brewery storage that could be seen when crossing the bridge from Holyoke into Chicopee. In 1933, after prohibition was repealed, Hampden opened under new ownership. In the 1940s, the company flourished with the sale of Hampden Mild Ale, which became one of New England's leading brands. In 1967, the company was sold to Piel's which ceased operation in 1975. Photograph courtesy of the Wistariahurst Museum Archives.

C. Adolf Voight came from Germany to work for Shreve, Crump & Lowe. His trade was that of a watch maker. He stood in front of his store on High Street in 1897. Photograph courtesy of the Wistariahurst Museum Archives

Hermann Bosback was born in Hueckeswagen on the Rhine in Germany. He came to Holyoke in 1895 and worked at the Germania Mills. Later, after establishing himself as a leading German citizen in Holyoke, he opened the Mt. Tom French Dry Cleaning Works at 146 Brown Avenue. The business started slowly but grew to be one of the best equipped plants in Massachusetts. They specialized in French dry cleaning, and the ladies of Holyoke gave him valuable laces, evening and opera gowns, and other apparel to clean.

Holyoke National Bank, c. late 1800s. Photograph courtesy of the Wistariahurst Museum Archives.

Banks were another important infrastructure of the city's economy. The first banking institution in Holyoke was the Hadley Falls Bank, organized in 1851. Its original capital was $100,000. The bank reorganized in 1865 as Hadley Falls National Bank. Another bank, the Holyoke National Bank, was organized in 1872 with William Whiting as its first president. In 1884, with a capital stock of $250,000 and president J.H. Newton, the Home National Bank was incorporated. Also in 1872, the Mechanics Savings Bank, located on 13 Dwight Street, was incorporated. People's Bank was incorporated in 1885 by James E. Delaney, Moses Newton, John Tilly, and James Ranger. They elected William Skinner as first Presi-

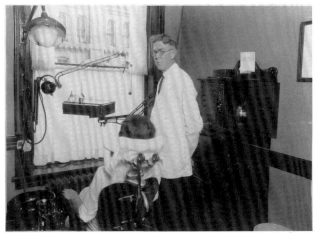

Dr. Edward Mayo, of Irish descent, received his degree from Pennsylvania College of Dental Medicine and Dental Surgery in 1901. Though he first moved into practice in Springfield, by 1903, he moved his dental office to 380 High Street. Photograph courtesy of the Wistariahurst Museum Archives.

Market that sells groceries. Photograph courtesy of the Holyoke Public Library History Room.

dent. It originally occupied a space in Home National Bank, which was located in the Tilly Block opposite of City Hall. The bank moved to the corner of High and Appleton Streets in 1901. In 1917, People's moved to 365 High Street. Its first branch opened on Pleasant Street in 1966.

Puerto Ricans, Holyoke's most recent group to find work and settle in the city, began arriving in the late 1950s. Unlike early immigrant groups who came to Holyoke during periods of expanding population and economy, the Puerto Ricans came when the existing population was in decline. The bulk of the job opportunities for Puerto Ricans were in seasonal labor in the tobacco industry. The Puerto Ricans settled in Holyoke at a time when the city had fewer low skilled jobs. This made it more difficult for the newcomers to experience the upward mobility that other immigrant groups found in the city's manufacturing industry.

Besides working in the service industry, Puerto Ricans have a solid place in Holyoke's commercial life. As was the case with the other groups that came to Holyoke, the Puerto Ricans have set up ethnic stores and restaurants like Fernandes Family Restaurant and Salsarengue, which serve traditional and authentic Puerto Rican food.

Antonio Robles, who worked for Worthington Pump Company as a laborer and a fork lift operator, remembered his experiences when he first migrated to Holyoke: "So many people think just because you are Puerto Rican, you are not reliable and will go back to Puerto Rico. But I like it here. It has a nice atmosphere for families, its away from the noisy city."

When the Holyoke Mall at Ingleside opened in 1979, Holyoke citizens fears were realized and downtown Holyoke was no longer a center for retail business. Another significant factor in the decline of downtowns nationwide was the movement of families to the suburbs after World War II. However, the mall created a huge infusion of tax revenues and plenty of employment opportunities in the service sector.

Perpetual Help Church on Chestnut Street. Photograph courtesy of the Holyoke Public Library History Room.

Holyoke's Religious Communities

"motorists approaching Paper City over the range..have their eye arrested by....a massive square tower, bearing aloft a cross and below the tower a cruciform church."

Religion was an important part of everyday life outside of Holyoke's workplace. As had been true in the 1850s, there was little diversion outside religious group activities. Sundays and sometimes once during the week, many of Holyoke's population went to church. On feast days, Irish and French Canadian Catholics went to Mass. Fraternal organizations like the Fenians, the German Benevolent Society, St. Jerome's Temperance, Benevolent and Literary Society, or the Societe de St. Jean Baptiste celebrated with church dances and picnics. The churches and synagogues were the center of social life in Holyoke, with church socials and fairs among the principle gatherings for newcomers and old friends.

A brochure about the location of a Catholic church in Holyoke described "motorists approaching Paper City over the range.... have their eye arrested by a specific object in the landscape. Heart and mind, if as sensitive as the eye, have been arrested too. The object is a massive square tower, bearing aloft a cross

First Congregational Church in Ireland Parish. Image courtesy of Holyoke Public Library History Room.

and below the tower a cruciform church. Facing the town, then, we face this supreme symbol, the Cross, on its hill top. Below it, on all sides, the city. Behind it, miles of valley, bounded by hill-ranges against the sky." The church referred to was Blessed Sacrament, in Ward 6.

Many of the immigrant groups to Holyoke were Roman Catholic, while the native or Yankee residents of Holyoke were mostly Protestant. The churches associated with Protestants included the First Baptist Church, the Second Baptist Church, the Bethlehem Community, First Congregational Church, Second Congregational Church, Grace Congregational, Evangelical Lutheran, the First Methodist Church, the African Methodist Episcopal Church, First Presbyterian, St. Paul's Episcopal, St. Luke's Mission, the Reformed Church in the United States, the Salvation Army, Gospel Hall, the Polish Evangelistic Assembly, the Polish Bible Study, the Jehovah's Witnesses and the Unitarian Church.

Roman Catholic Churches in Holyoke included those for English speakers: St. Jerome's, Sacred Heart, Holy Rosary, Holy Cross, Holy Family and Blessed Sacrament; those for French speakers: Precious Blood, Perpetual Help, and Immaculate Conception; those for the Polish speaking: Mater Dolorosa; and St. Michel's Greek Orthodox Church for those who spoke Greek.

In 1899, the Paper City Lodge of the Order Brith Abraham provided religious, fraternal and protective services to the small yet growing Jewish community of Holyoke.

Religious Groups in Holyoke by Social Class, 1947

Labor Churches

Protestant: Bethlehem Community, Baptist, Grace Congregational, Evangelical Lutheran, Reformed, Gospel Hall, Jehovah's Witness, Polish Evangelistic Assembly, Polish Bible Study Group, Salvation Army

Catholic: Holy Family, Holy Rosary, Immaculate Conception, Mater Dolorosa, Precious Blood, St. Michael, St. Jerome's

Middle Class Churches

Protestant: First Baptist Church, Second Baptist Church, Methodist Church, Presbyterian Church

Catholic: Sacred Heart, Perpetual Help

Upper Middle Class Churches

Protestant: First Congregational, Second Congregational, Episcopal

Catholic: Holy Cross, Blessed Sacrament

Interestingly, Kenneth Underwood's research on Protestant and Catholicism in Holyoke leads to the observation that there were certain churches for different classes of people.

The First Orthodox Congregational Church, originally a meeting house built in 1834 in Ireland Parish, was formed by Reverend Dr. Lathrop in 1799. The Irish families that settled in the Holyoke area after in the 1800s were mostly from northern Ireland and were of Protestant faith. Its original members included Joseph Rogers, Amos Allen, Titus Morgan, Timothy Clough, Lucas Morgan, Nathan Stevens, Jonathan Clough, John Miller and Grover Street.

In the early 1800s, Thomas Rand established the First Baptist Church and became its first pastor.

The Second Congregational Church was organized in the spring of 1849 for Congregationalists who lived in Ireland Parish. The services were held in Lyman Street School, near the Lyman Mills. A church was built in 1852 at High and Dwight Streets. A larger church was built in 1886 at Maple and Appleton Streets.

The Second Baptist Church was built in 1849, with forty two members. Holyoke's Episcopal Church was also established in 1849 at the office of Mr. Fayette Smith, who was a justice of the peace. This church was later named the Trinity Church. It was abandoned only four months later as interest decreased. There was not an effort to establish another Episcopal Church until 1863 when St. Paul's Church was dedicated at Maple and Suffolk. The cornerstone was laid in 1866.

Before 1853, Methodists attended services at South Hadley Falls. It was not until 1853 that the Methodist Episcopal Church was established by Reverend Thomas Marcy. He preached in Lyceum Hall on the Exchange Block on High Street. Later, the "Old Methodist Church" was established at the corner of Main and Appleton Streets, dedicated in 1870.

The Methodist Church was located at Appleton and Elm Streets. It was torn down in 1970. Photograph courtesy of the Wistariahurst Museum Archives.

St. Jerome's Church, c. late 1880s. Photograph courtesy of the Wistariahurst Museum Archives.

St. Paul's Church, Holyoke, Mass.

St. Paul's Church, located at Appleton and Locust Streets, was finished in 1905. Photograph courtesy of the Wistariahurst Museum Archives.

Many mid-century Irish Catholic immigrants had not been to Mass or taken the sacraments for years and only became closely affiliated with the Catholic Church after arriving in America. Father Jeremiah O'Callaghan came to Holyoke from County Cork Ireland in 1854, and established Holyoke's first parish Church, St. Jerome's. It was erected in 1856 but was not completed until 1860. Father O'Callaghan spoke fluent Gaelic and delivered sermons in his native tongue. Our Lady of the Rosary was set apart from St. Jerome's in 1886 and built a new church a year later on what was known as the Ely Lot.

French Canadians soon discovered that Franco-American parishes offered services in French as well as social activities not unlike the ones they had at home. These parishes often constituted havens that enabled recent immigrants to adapt to the living and working conditions of the time.

As the number of Franco-Americans grew in New England and parishes were established, parishioners founded their own schools in order to provide what they considered proper training and education. Their beliefs were that losing the French language was tantamount to abandoning the Catholic faith. Two lay-women in 1869 who Holyoke attended convent schools in Canada were recruited to teach at these schools.

Prior to the building of the first French parish, Precious Blood, in 1869, the French Canadian population of Holyoke worshiped at St. Jerome's Church. Reverend Dufresne organized a new parish on Park Street,

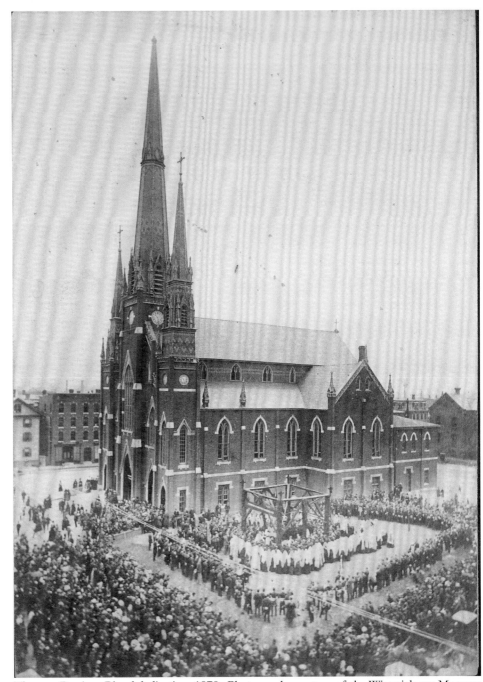

The new Precious Blood dedication, 1878. Photograph courtesy of the Wistariahurst Museum Archives.

Postcard of the German Evangelical Church. Photograph courtesy of the Holyoke Public Library History Room.

dedicated in 1870 as Church of the Precious Blood. As it had been in Canada, the Catholic Church quickly became the focus of social life in French Canadian enclaves. At church-sponsored activities, French Canadians obtained a respite from their arduous daily activities, exchanged family and neighborhood news, and met people. They watched minstrel shows, musical presentations, and plays, and performed in theater clubs. At 5 PM on May 27, 1875, fire broke out during Corpus Christi devotions in a crowded temporary chapel of Precious Blood parish. 97 people died. A new building on Cabot and Park Streets was dedicated in 1878.

In 1890 it was necessary to create a second French Catholic Parish, Our Lady of Perpetual Help, and in 1903 a third, The Immaculate Conception. Our Lady of Perpetual Help was a newer Catholic Church with a school, church and auditorium associated with it. To immigrants of the first generation, the church reminded them of their towns at home, with their customs, relatives and friends. A French Congregational Church was established in 1884 by Reverend Mr. Cote and served as a general missionary for the French Congregational workers.

When new citizens were coming into Holyoke from Ireland and Canada, it became necessary to erect another church for English speaking Catholics. On Maple and Sergeant Streets, Sacred Heart's cornerstone was dedicated on Independence Day of 1876. The first mass was Christmas day. Two more parishes, the Holy Rosary in the Flats and Holy Cross in the Highlands, were dedicated in 1886 and 1905 respectively.

In 1867, the small German Evangelical Lutheran Church was built on Jackson Street between Park and

Presbyterian Church of Holyoke. Photograph courtesy of the
Wistariahurst Museum Archives.

Interior of the Second Congregational Church. Photograph courtesy of the
Wistariahurst Museum Ar-
chives.

84

Aerial photograph of Mater Dolorosa, 1930s. Photograph courtesy of the Holyoke Public Library History Room.

South Bridge Streets. With the help of August Stursberg, one of the owners of the Germania Mills, they practiced High Church, which was worship according to the ritualistic forms of the Lutheran Church in the motherland, and was attractive to all who understood the German language. The first leader of the church was Reverend M. Frankel.

The German Reformed Church was organized in 1892. German immigrants felt the need to reach a large unchurched mass of German immigrants in the area.

In 1874, the Unity Church began as the quaint Liberty Church that had been organized as early as 1849. It was short lived, however, until the Holyoke Water Power Company donated the land on the corner of Maple and Essex Street to build a new church. The congregation banded together and avowed the purpose of "maintaining public worship and advocating piety and good morals under the name of the Unitarian Society of Holyoke." In 1888, the Presbyterian Church was built on a lot secured from Holyoke Water Power Company on the corner of Cabot and Chestnut Streets. Because churches were a main source of social connection for many immigrants and migrants, choirs and children's after school groups formed at the churches. This was, of course, in addition to social functions like dances.

The Polish immigrants were the last to establish a colony and form a national church. The Polish Catholic Church was created as Polish immigrants streamed into Holyoke in the 1890s. Mater Dolorosa, located at the corner of Lyman and Maple Streets, continues to have devoted parishioners since its construction was completed in 1903.

The Jews came for opportunity and religious freedom and set up small shops. They did not end up creating distinct communities, but did maintain close ties through their synagogues. On average, 25 Jewish families came to Holyoke a year. In 1890, four families entered Holyoke, while in 1906, there were 140. The Russian and Polish Jews came to Holyoke as early as 1883. There was no Jewish congregation until 1891 because Hebrew Law stated that there must be at least 10 heads of families to form a congregation. The first congregation of Russian Jews was Agudas Achim, Society of Brothers. It was changed to B'nai Zion, Congregation of the Sons of Zion in 1902. The congregation recruited from a seminary that trained rabbis to conduct festivals at Yom Kippur. By 1904, the Jewish community of

Formerly Grace Congregational Church, the Christian Pentacostal Church on Race and Cabot Streets today serves mostly Puerto Rican residents of Holyoke. Photograph taken in 2006.

Holyoke wanted a more strict Orthodox congregation. They built a synagogue in South Holyoke called Rodphey Sholom.

Puerto Rican migrants began setting up store front churches downtown. For example, La Casa Maria is a Pentecostal group associated with the Catholic Church and Urban Ministries. Catholic Puerto Ricans attend La Casa Maria, Spanish Apostolate, while Protestant Puerto Ricans attend the Christian Pentecostal Church, which was formed in 1967.

Storefront church on Dwight Street near City Hall. Photograph taken in 2006.

The Catholic Church responded to each of the national groups in a different way because their needs varied greatly. In general, the French and Polish sought to use the resources of the Church to maintain national beliefs and manners within the parish and neighborhood. The presence of a huge number of people from Ireland, French Canada and Poland made it possible to perpetuate ethnic traditions and loyalties.

Religious associations often reflected particular approaches to society. Catholic associations included the Catholic Girls' League, Catholic Hospital Alumnae Association, the Catholic High School Athletic Association, the Catholic Polish Veterans group, the Catholic Veterans, Catholic Scouts, and the Knights of Columbus. Protestant groups were less in number and included the Protestant Girls' Association and the Protestant Junior Girls' Association.

The first institution of Catholic culture was the Holyoke Catholic Mutual Benevolent Society, founded in 1857. The society provided sick members $3 a week, unless the illness was "induced by intemperance or other immorality." Irishman Maurice Lynch, well known as Vice President of the St. Jerome's Temperance Society, first worked as an apprentice to brick makers in Holyoke. He then operated a grocery store and then formed a contracting business with his brothers. St. Jerome's also built St. Jerome's High School

YMCA. Photograph courtesy of the Wistariahurst Museum Archives.

The YMCA wrestling team for the year 1927-1928. Bottom row: ?, Owner Brill, Cliff White, ?, ?. Top row: Manager, Earl Cawkins, Tommy Rae, Scotty Richie, ?, ?, Coach Ernie Rosseau. Photograph courtesy of Holyoke Public Library History Room.

St. Jerome's High School, class of 1925. Photograph courtesy of the Wistariahurst Museum Archives.

and the Temperance Association. Many immigrants were more comfortable keeping company in the culture and community familiar to them.

The Ancient Order of the Hibernians was the first organization in Ireland established when penal laws considered the use of the Irish language a felony. The Ancient Order of the Hibernians Division I was founded in Holyoke in February of 1872 with Valentine J. O'Donnell as the first president. They met at Union Hall on Maple Street and moved to Parsons then Straton's Hall on High Street. In 1925, the Order was so strong in Holyoke that the national convention was held in the Paper City. The associational lives of the Irish middle class centered around the Catholic Church and its lay associations, the Democratic Party, and such Irish nationalist organizations as the Ancient Order of Hibernians and the Land League. Through picnics, parades, meetings, and torchlight processions, the Land League advanced the cause of a free Ireland and served as an important center of social activity.

There were two chapters of Fenians in Holyoke, the Irish Lion Circle and the O'Neil Circle. These men were loyal to their brotherhood in Ireland who were fighting for independence from England. In the late 1860s, the Fenians drilled behind Exchange Hall. During the St. Patrick's Parade, they donned green jackets trimmed with orange braids and blue pants with a white cap. The fateful year of 1869 gave the Fenian's a history most would remember. Two raids were made in an attempt to invade British ruled Canada. However, the bloodless defeat of the expedition would go down in history.

St. Jerome's Temperance Society, 1888. Photograph courtesy of the Wistariahurst Museum Archives.

Distressed by the immorality of the saloons, a group of young men in 1866 created a social center to rival the saloons. This social center eventually became the Young Men's Christian Association. Organized by Protestant church members in 1885, the YMCA was to bring young men under moral and religious influences by introducing them to members and the privilege of the Association. The YMCA aided them in the selection of suitable boarding, places of employment, and by serving their attendance as a place of worship. There was also an evening school offered to immigrant boys who had to work during the day. It was at the YMCA in 1895 where William Morgan invented volleyball!

The Jewish community established the Young Men's Hebrew Athletic Association and the Young Women's Hebrew Association in 1913 in order to promote Zionism. The Hadassah was a group who made clothes for Palestinian children during World War I.

The German Reform Church organized two societies: The Young People's Society, the Ladies Aid Society,

Children's group at a German Church in South Holyoke. Photograph courtesy of the Holyoke Public Library History Room.

organized in 1893.

Quebecois brought with them institutions from French Canada which changed as the French community in Holyoke grew more acclimated to their new home. Early on, such groups were church-related and served primarily the leaders of the community. The St. Jean Baptiste Society is the oldest of French societies, first organized in April of 1872 and the Union of St. Joseph, founded in 1880, provided mutual insurance benefits and promoted national, ethnic and religious interests. With no formal relation to the church, French associations included Cercle Rochambeau and the Beavers Club.

German Evangelical Luthern Church Choir, c. 1911. The choir usually had at least 15 members. Photograph courtesy of the Holyoke Public Library History Room.

School girls walk home through an alley way behind Steigers and Childs in 1967. Photograph courtesy of the Holyoke Public Library History Room.

Recreation in Holyoke

"s'instruire at s'amuser"

Church, family, benevolent societies, and other institutions enriched the lives of Holyoke's working class. Within these institutions workers defined themselves and created a number of distinct cultural worlds. One world was of responsibility based on the duty to family inculcated from an early age, where young workers developed values necessary to maintain their families. After a long working day, for both merchant and mill worker, there was little time for recreation, except for the occasional entertainment, such as a concert, an exhibition of animals, or a choral performance. Organizations and recreational institutions provided solace from a long work week. Immigrants and migrants enriched the social and cultural character of the community in a way that is reflected in Holyoke today.

The laborers who built the dam and dug canals formed the backbone of saloon culture within the Irish community. When relaxing, they lingered for a time in the raucous, hard drinking world of the saloon. Saloon culture emerged as a separate working-class culture during the industrial revolution. As the initial wave of construction decline in Holyoke, many sought work at the mills, where they encountered a new industrial *morality*. The mill owners and capitalists who spearheaded the industrial revolution demanded more discipline. Apprentices received temperance medals rather than lessons on how to drink. Schools stressed hard work. In mid-century

Craft's Tavern postcard. Photograph courtesy of the Wistariahurst Museum Archives.

Craft's Tavern, c. 1920s, with Dan McCarthy standing on the stairs. Photograph courtesy of the Holyoke Public Library History Room.

Ye Olde BUD

Now's as good a time as any to enjoy The Bud!

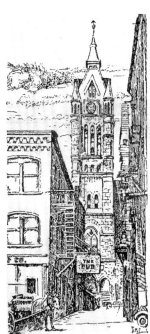

Once a back alley speakeasy, The Bud was known as a purveyor of "hooch." Legend says that the ghost of P.J. Murray, well known owner at one time, haunts The Bud. From the collection of Wistariahurst Museum.

1923

Agnes Jenne	Holyoke, Mass.
Fred Wilson	Holyoke, Mass.
Emily Patterson	Holyoke, Mass.
Harold Patterson	Holyoke, Mass.
Martha Miller	Holyoke, Mass.
Bessie Miller	Holyoke, Mass.
Grace Patterson	Holyoke, Mass.
Leonard Gibbons	Holyoke, Mass.
Robert Graham	Holyoke, Mass.
Florence Graham	Holyoke, Mass.
Mrs. Wm Graham	Holyoke, Mass.
Miss Rosella Andrews	Holyoke, Mass.
Mrs Jennie Andrews	Holyoke, Mass.
Miss Catherine O'Conner	Holyoke, Mass.
Mrs C. S. Chase	Holyoke, Mass.
Mr. H. B. Chandler	Holyoke, Mass.
Mrs. H. B. Chandler	Holyoke, Mass.
Dorothy Chandler	Holyoke, Mass.
Francis P. Earley	Holyoke, Mass.
Miss Jennie O'Connor	Holyoke, Mass.
Miss Catherine O'Connor	Springfield, Mass.
Mrs Helen Riley	Holyoke, Mass.
Mr. Daniel Riley	Holyoke, Mass.
Mary R. Riley	Holyoke, Mass.
Kitty Riley	Holyoke, Mass.
Michael Riley	Holyoke, Mass.
William J Riley	Holyoke, Mass.
Mary A Lynch	Holyoke, Mass.
Patrick Riley	Holyoke, Mass.
Marion L. Pelissier	Holyoke, Mass.
Lucy M. Champagne	Holyoke, Mass.
Helen M. Gray	City
Catherine M. Gray	City of Holyoke, Mass.
Mary B. Curley	Holyoke, Mass.

Holyoke, those immigrants who had only recently left pre-industrial southwestern counties of Ireland comprised the group most resistant to the new industrial morality. They went to the saloons and places like Craft's Tavern. The Tavern was built by Archibald Morgan in 1795 on Northampton Street in 1875. It closed in 1923 and is now the site of the John J. Lynch School.

This is a page from the Dedication sign-in book of Craft's Tavern in 1923. From the collection of Wistariahurst Museum.

The Holyoke Public Library was opened in 1870 with 300 patrons and 2,500 books. Because reading for pleasure was considered unworthy, library founders felt that if good books were not provided for the young, they might read novels and sensational newspapers! The first location of the library was in a room in the old Appleton Street School. In 1876, the library moved to a central room on the main floor of City Hall. In 1897, Holyoke Water Power Company offered the library a city block, where the library stands today.

The Holyoke Music Club held its first meeting on Saturday, March 16, 1889 at Fanny Reed's house. There were six members present. At each meeting, a member would present a paper on a specific composer, like Bach or Beethoven. Also, "Miss Newton played for us 'The Funeral March' which was very much enjoyed. Chocolate and cake

Postcard of the Holyoke Public Library. Photograph courtesy of the Wistariahurst Museum Archives.

Programme

le 16 Octobre 1967

Hotesses: Mesdames Bernier et Madame Martin.

"Une saison dans la vie d'Emmanuel"
par Marie-Claire Blais. Madame Lavoie.

"Midi Minuit" par Jean Cayrol. Madame Arthur Hebert.

le 13 Novembre 1967

Hotesses: Mesdames Arthur Herbert et Alfred Lavoie.

"Celeste Mogador" par Pierre de Gorffe. Madame Martin.

"Le feux de la Chandeleur".
par Catherine Payran. Madame Bernier.

le 11 Decembre 1967

Hotesses: Mesdames Barsalou et Rene Hebert.

"La Palmeraie" par Francois-Regis Bastide. Madame Denys.

"L'air de Venise" par Solange Fasquelle. Madame LaRochelle.

le 12 Fevrier 1968

Hotesses: Mesdames Chartier et Rogers.

"Les deux cotes de la mer" par Armand Hoog. Madame Potvin.

Programme (suite)

"Les Quatre Murs" par Michel Ragon. Madames Rene Hebert.

le 11 Mars 1968

Hotesses: Mesdames Potvin et Burgee.

"L'Homme de la Colline"
par Marie-Anne Desmarest. Madame Chartier.

"L'Ete Finit sous les Tilleuls"
par Kleber Haedens. Madame J. Wilbur Murray.

le 15 Avril 1968

Hotesses: Mesdames Murray et Larochelle.

"Oblier Parlerme"
par Edmonde Charles' Roux. Madame Burgee.

"La Vie Quotidienne" des Comedies de Moliere.
par Georges Mongredien. Madome Rogers.

le 13 Mai 1968

Hotesses: Mesdames Barsalou et A. Omer Hebert.

"Beau Francois" par Maurice Genevoix. Madame Barsalou.

"Les Aveux Infideles"
par Jacques de Bourbon Busset. Madame A. Omer Hebert.

Le Cercle Litteraire Francais program 1867-1868. From the collection of Wistariahurst Museum.

Hampden Park. Photograph courtesy of the Holyoke Public Library History Room.

were served." People of all ethnic backgrounds were welcome in the Music Club.

The French community in Holyoke supported a number of social and fraternal groups, and these, too, changed with time. Early on, such groups were church-related and served primarily the leaders of the community. After 1885, dozens of new organizations were formed and with few exceptions, their aims and purposes were decidedly secular. The motto of the Cercle Rochambeau, 1900, was "s'instruire at s'amuser" or "to instruct and amuse oneself." A social hall was built in Ward 6 for these French organizations in 1885.

Parks and other open recreational areas were created for after work and after school activities. The Riverside Park wading pool was located on Joseph Prew's Riverside Track. The track no longer exists but Springdale Park is a busy recreational park. At the intersection of Park and South Bridge Streets was the Germania Park, established in 1853 for German migrants who worked at the Germania Mills. Their Lutheran Church and school were both located across from the park. Prospect Park overlooks the Connecti-

A couple sits at Elmwood Park. Photograph courtesy of the Holyoke Public Library History Room.

cut River in Ward 6.

Auggie Monty remembers her "playground was Prospect Park where we roller skated and played hide-and-seek among the trees. The stone wall was a favorite place to walk along to view our dam and the Connecticut River. If one was allowed to swim, we enjoyed the pool at the far end of the park. We played hop scotch in front of our home making the hop scotch in white chalk."

The League of American Wheelmen in Holyoke. Photograph courtesy of the Wistariahurst Museum Archives.

The League of American Wheelmen in Holyoke was a club for those who were interested in bicycling. In 1896 when Charles E. Walker opened up his Sporting Goods Store on High Street in Holyoke. The first big bicycle boom hit the country at the same time. His grandson, Roy Walker Jr. took over running the store. When he pedaled the streets of Holyoke, he usually carried a set of wrenches – for the unexpected adjustments. Edward L. Outterson, pictured at right, moved to Holyoke, in the late 1870s. Edward was a papermaker by trade and worked at a number of Holyoke's paper manufacturers including Whiting Paper Company, the Connecticut River Paper Company and the Crocker Manufacturing Company. His hobby was bicycle riding and racing. He rode in and won many

prizes and medals. He was a member of the Holyoke Bicycle Club and the League of American Wheelmen. Up until the 1920s, bicycles were vehicles enjoyed by adults only. By the 1950s, bikes were for kids only and the industry was fighting to stay afloat.

In the downtown area, there were many activities for relaxing and enjoying oneself after work. Holyoke's Opera House, located at the corner of Front and John Streets, adjacent to the Windsor Hotel, was built by William Whiting and opened in 1878. It was the stop for touring companies out of New York City. Sadly, it closed in 1955 and burned in 1967.

There were a few halls where Holyokers showed off their dance moves or learned to dance. One French Canadian remembered how she "used to go dancing at Kelly's Dance Hall on Dwight Street. Sometimes on Tuesday night, Thursday and Saturday and when I went dancing….we had a model-T Ford where all us girls, my sister drove it, we'd all go together. Then after if we went different places, mostly we'd go to the same dance hall but a lot of times they'd go different places, some would probably go to this place across from the Victory Theater [to a ballroom], and sometimes some of my sisters would go there and then we'd meet, ….or sometimes my brother would pick us up because the trolley cars stopped at twelve at night."

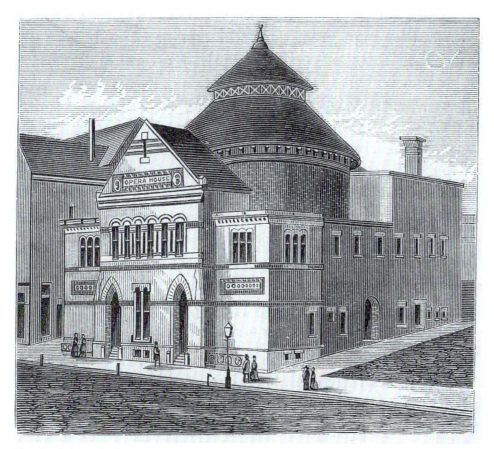

Regina Loughran, first generation French Canadian, said that the people she worked with were a mix of French Canadian,

Sketch of the Holyoke Opera House. Image courtesy of the Wistariahurst Museum Archives.

San Sauci Club House, pictured above in 1890, had an annual regatta on the Connecticut River. Photograph courtesy of the Wistariahurst Museum Archives.

Polish, German and Irish and that they socialized outside the mills as well as inside the mills. "They'd get together sometimes. Like on Saturdays, they'd go for hikes, we'd go for long walks and we had a lot of fun… oh yes…of course, when you're young you make your own fun. We'd go dancing. I loved to dance. I learned in there, in Skinners [mill]. Sometimes, we'd go in the bathroom and I'd just say to the girls, 'How do you do this step? How do you do that step? And for a couple of minutes… why sometimes you had to wait to get in, there were so many in there…so it gave us a chance and that's how I learned."

Every year there was a regatta at the San Sauci Club House (which later became the Holyoke Canoe Club), located north of Holyoke. The Canoe Club, incorporated in 1888, began small. Thomas Auld, Jr., a lifetime member of the Canoe Club, remembered that "the first Holyoke Canoe Club was a little storage thing down by the dam that held six to eight canoes, and that was the Holyoke Canoe Club."

The club moved several times, with the final club house built at Smith's Ferry in 1903, where it remains today. Holyoke's third generation found social life more unified than it had been, but

Canoe Club sailing on the Connecticut River in 1890s. Photograph courtesy of the Wistariahurst Museum Archives.

there were still some separation between Protestants and Catholics. Excluded fairly consistently from membership in the Canoe Club, Irish, French Canadians and Poles organized outing clubs with headquarters in places just beyond the city limits like Hampden Ponds.

German religious and cultural organizations furthered the self-sufficiency of their community. Among the mutual benefit societies founded by national groups in Holyoke, the German Benevolent Society, established in the 1860s. Germans also cultivated interest in music, and on several occasions German societies

Gymnasium at the Springdale Turnverein. Photograph courtesy of the Holyoke Public Library History Room.

gave concerts and hosted festivals. The Turnverein, founded in the 1870s, were perhaps the most active and powerful. The Turnverein originated as a systematic gymnastic training and was as much a part of German life as church-going. In the Turn Halles, like the one originally located at 624 South Bridge Street, people could recreate in gymnasiums and congregate at beer halls. For example, on October 5, 1965, the Turnverein had a good, old fashion Schlachfest with food, music and dancing.

In the late 1800s, neighborhood welfare institutions or settlement houses, became popular throughout the United States. They were established in growing working communities to assist working class women. The Skinner Coffee House is an example of such a place. Created in 1902 by Belle and

The Turnvereins were noted for their gymnastic facilities, like this one in South Holyoke. Many talented gymnasts came out of these Turnvereins. The facing page shows a member practicing. Above shows four members of a gymnastic team. Photographs courtesy of Shirley Morrison.

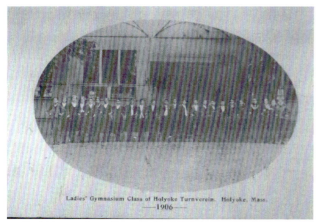

Ladies' Gymnasium Class of Holyoke Turnverein. Holyoke, Mass.
——1906——

Ladies' Gymnasium Class at the Turnverein in Holyoke, 1906. Photograph courtesy of the Holyoke Public Library History Room.

German Shooting Club, 1908 at Hampden Ponds. Max Giehler is in the second row, sixth from the right. He immigrated from Germany in the mid 1800s and eventually worked as a weaver in Holyoke. Photograph courtesy of the Holyoke Public Library History Room.

Katharine Skinner in remembrance of their father William Skinner, the Coffee House opened its doors to women of all race, color, religion, and *land of origin*. This gathering place provided food at nominal fees, educational classes, and social gatherings for the workers of the local mills and their daughters. The aim was to improve neighborhood life and create a solid community for women. There were over 20 clubs and organizations associated with the Skinner Coffee House. Along with providing entertainment through pageants and musical revues, organizations created a community through regularly scheduled meetings and luncheons. Many girls joined the same clubs years after their mothers' involvement, indicating stability of the organization and strong family and ethnic ties. Some of the clubs at the Skinner Coffee House

Sally Johnson, program assistant Margaret Fallon, Iris Cruz, Judy Lopen and Katie Healy wait for a bus to take them to the Springfield Museums in 1975. Photograph courtesy of the Wistariahurst Museum Archives.

The Mother's Club met at the Skinner Coffee House often, as they did in this photo taken in 1919. Photograph courtesy of the Wistariahurst Museum Archives.

included: Women's Club, French-American Club, Association for the Blind, Italian Women's Club, Home-makers Club, Negro Women's Club, Polish Women's Club, Children's Dramatic Club, Junior Reading Group, Polish Folk Dance Group, Children's Glee Club, Ukrainian Women's Club, Quilt Club and the Dancing Club.

The Women's Club was the largest club at the Skinner Coffee House. It was known for organizing activities like Musical Revues, luncheons, and pageants. Anita Marcotte Healey, of French Canadian descent and the former director of the Skinner Coffee House said "We had French, German, Italian, Negro [using the Coffee House]. Its all-American a mixture of everyone. There were Irish, too, but they were not as classified as much. The Women's Club were a mixture too. Most of the French moved out in the 1960s. [Before that time] the French were predominant users of the building."

The Italian Progressive Society, a mutual help group, was formed in 1900. The club's aim was to help local Italians employed in the mills and in shops against the loss of income in case of illness and accidents. The club met at various homes on the first Monday of each month. The Sons of Italy organized in 1926 as a local lodge part of an international group that raised money used to help persons of Italian descent throughout the world. The Holyoke group helped support an

The Italian Women's Club, who often met at the Skinner Coffee House in the 1960s, shown here having dinner before their New York trip to the Latin Quarter. Photograph courtesy of Pauline Giusti Walton.

Cooking Club of Holyoke, December 1889. Photograph courtesy of the Wistariahurst Museum Archives.

Italian rest home outside of Boston, an orphanage in Italy, and gave scholarships to local youth.

The Kocziusczko Club was organized in the 1893 by early Polish immigrants as a mutual benefit association to help members during times of illness and death. It transformed into a social club and then took shape as a non-profit corporation that established the Holyoke Polish Home and the Kocziusczko Building that housed the numerous Polish societies and clubs.

Crowds gather to listen to a concert at Mountain Park in 1905. Photograph courtesy of the Wistariahurst Museum Archives.

Many immigrants saved up their money to take the trolley to Mountain Park. The amusement park was established by the Holyoke Street Railway in 1895 as a Trolley Park. The trolleys would park near the carousel. There were water rides, stages for concerts and landscaped areas for recreation such as the live theater, a carousel and a roller coaster. The Casino Playhouse was built in 1901 and hosted performers such as Hal Holbrook, Lloyd Bridges and Caesar Romero. A second generation French Canadian remembered the "One time ..... all the factories had a play at the Casino at Mountain Park...... And every factory in Holyoke, that is American Thread, the Alpaca, Skinners and I think the other one was the American

There was a trolley that began downtown Holyoke and shuttled many Holyokers to Mountain Park for the evening or all day on a weekend. This photo was taken c. 1930. Photograph courtesy of the Wistariahurst Museum Archives.

Writing, National Blank Book I think it was. They each…their own company had a play at the Casino. I forget…I think it was to raise money, I think. And I was in it. I was a Spanish dancer in that. I'll never forget it [laughter]. Oh we rehearsed for that but it was fun. It was really fun. And the Skinners came to the play and they sat way down the front and I can just see them clapping. They were regular people. They were nice people, you know. *THAT* I remember about them." Eugenie Cote, second generation French Canadian, said that despite working hard all day, she and the others had enough energy left to go dancing at Mountain Park in the evening. Annie Kane, Irish born, said of Mountain Park, "I went into the Hadley [Thread] Mill to work at 14 for $6 a week, six to six, as a doffer. We had to all pitch in. [to help our families]. Out of $6 I got fifty cents – I used to save that to go dancing. That was big in them days – you could go to Mountain Park for five cents."

In 1929, the park was expanded and the amusement rides of Mt. Wildcat roller coaster and the Philadelphia Toboggan Carousel were built, along with a road for automobiles to get up to the park. 1987 was the

Riding the Carousel. Photograph courtesy of the Holyoke Public Library History Room.

Members of the Mountain Park Opera Company pose for a photograph advertising their 130th performance of the season, 1901. Photograph courtesy of the Wistariahurst Museum Archives.

It was worth the wait to purchase custard at this stand at Mountain Park. Photograph courtesy of the Wistariahurst Museum Archives.

Children enjoy the Dodgems ride at Mountain Park. Photograph courtesy of the Holyoke Public Library History Room.

year of the sad announcement that, due to the retirement of Roger Fortin, the operations manager, the park would close after the season. However, in 1993, after fundraising and with the help of the City of Holyoke, the 48 horse carousel moved to Heritage State park and opened to the public.

Sports, both organized and unorganized, remained a large part of recreation for Holyokers of all ages. Fighters like John Scully, whose dream in life was to go "bare knuckles to a finish, for a purse of $25 or $50 a side" with a South Hadley Falls slugger named Hickey, could find ready support in the city's saloons. Outdoors, unorganized fighting and gang membership constituted an important part of growing up for working class youth. Gangs were established on a clear basis, as rival groups of Irish and French Canadians regularly beat each other senseless on the streets.

As early as 1860 there were two rival ball clubs in Holyoke, though the game they played was not modern baseball. After the Civil War, more teams sprang

Holyoke B. B. C., 1875. Back row, left to right: C. Farrington (Manager), William Sullivan (CF), J.T. Lynch (LF), J. Lynch (RF), D. O'Neil (SS), P. Moore (sub), and E. Whiting (Manager.) Front row, left to right: F. Syner (3 B), R. Winchester (2 B, Capt.), J. Bergh (C), and T. Donovan (1 B). Photograph courtesy of the Wistariahurst Museum Archives.

Holyoke Baseball Champions of 1901. Photograph courtesy of the Holyoke Public Library History Room.

There was also a little league for boys who wanted to play baseball like their hometown heroes. Photograph courtesy of the Wistariahurst Museum Archives.

up as the sport became the American National Pastime: High school versus grammar school, Lyman Mills cotton team versus Lyman Mills repair shop team, Meteors versus Monitors, Flats versus the Hill.

A female French Canadian who worked in the Skinner Silk Mills remembered that they "had a girl's basketball team. A good one! The Farr Alpaca had one. The American Thread had one and they used to play one another. And they'd play sometimes Easthampton girls or from Springfield and they were very good...." Another worker from Skinners, Desire DeVries, second generation French Canadian, said "They beat the best out in the middle

Holyoke's 1912 Volleyball team. Photograph courtesy of the Wistariahurst Museum Archives.

Here, a noontime concert July 3, 1919 at Deane Works (Worthington) included a duet by Messrs Foote and Bailey. Photograph courtesy of the Wistariahurst Museum Archives.

west…yeah, they [the Skinner Mills] paid for everything. It was more or less for advertising, you know."

Mill owners promoted camaraderie among their workers. Jones Davis, an agent of the Lyman Mills, made a special effort to create more community among his mill employees. He organized Christmas parties and sleigh rides for his employees, all at the expense of the Lyman Mill Company. The Farr Alpaca Company

Deane Shop's Bowling Champions, from Department 13, 1918-1919. Photograph courtesy of Pauline Giusti Walton.

Farr Alpaca Brass Band celebrating its 50th anniversary. Photograph courtesy of the Holyoke Public Library History Room.

Helen Wagner, born in Whatley, Massachusetts, moved to Holyoke and began working at Farr Alpaca when she was eighteen years old. She starred in a play in Farr Alpaca's auditorium. The Farr Alpaca Mill put on many different kinds of shows, including musicals and dramatic pieces. Photographs courtesy of the Wagner Family.

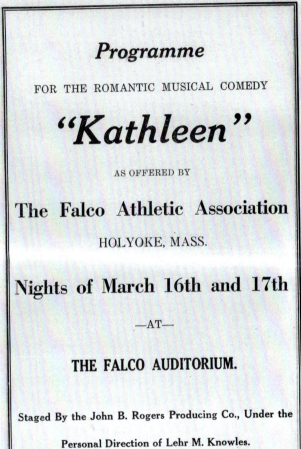

Programme

FOR THE ROMANTIC MUSICAL COMEDY

"*Kathleen*"

AS OFFERED BY

The Falco Athletic Association

HOLYOKE, MASS.

Nights of March 16th and 17th

—AT—

THE FALCO AUDITORIUM.

Staged By the John B. Rogers Producing Co., Under the

Personal Direction of Lehr M. Knowles.

was one of the largest employers in Holyoke and workers raved about what a good place it was to work. Farr Alpaca's band often practiced near the Winter Palace Roller Skating Rink in a large building near the underpass on Hampden Street.

More recently, Puerto Rican migrants have developed their own social groups, often around the family, the

Reikaldo Velazquez works on the community garden at Maple Street, c. 1970s. Photograph courtesy of the Holyoke Public Library History Room.

Children find activities to do outside, like breakdancing, as is the young man above. Photograph courtesy of the Holyoke Public Library History Room.

church and educational institutions. Nueva Esperanza, Inc. is a community development corporation in Holyoke that promotes development in housing, economics and human services. The organization's primary interest of providing affordable housing has expanded widely to include: neighborhood economic development, health and human service programs, development of community leadership, promotion of accessible community education and several youth empowerment programs. Nueva Esperanza's youth programs include El Arco Iris, YouthRap and YouthBuild.

Jose Rodriguez, a Puerto Rican native and resident of Holyoke, works for Nuestra Raices. Of his job, he

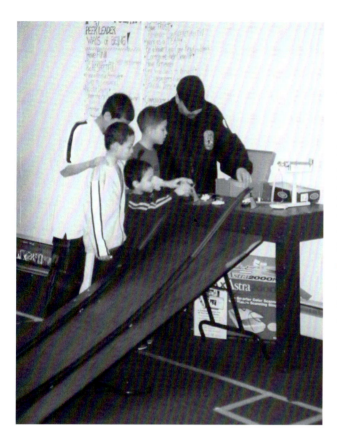

Young adults hang out at Nueva Esperanza, 2002.

says, "I feel very much a part of the community here in Holyoke. It doesn't matter if you're black, white, or another color - if you need help, we are here to help."

La Familia Hispana, Inc. sponsors the Annual Hispanic Family Festival in Springdale Park. The group's purpose is to foster community betterment for all people of Holyoke, with special emphasis on the Hispanic community and on youth. Their events and programs foster enrichment and development of the Hispanic culture and civic knowledge. This includes developing a library of Hispanic literature and films, and collaborating with other civil and cultural organizations.

La Familia Hispana's Festival at Springdale in July, 2006.

119

Civil Rights Parade in the 1960s downtown Holyoke. Photograph courtesy of the Holyoke Public Library History Room.

Holyoke's Culture and Identity

"The art, folklore, music.... our custom of sharing, our brotherhood bring us together. For all of these, I am very proud."

Some Americans who come from immigrant ancestors no longer identify with a particular ethnic group, while others strongly identify with their ethnic heritage. There are an increasing number of people of mixed ethnic and racial parentage who define their identity primarily from their occupation, consumer habits, generation, residential location and cultural lifestyle. Holyoke's cultural heritage holds an even more powerful story than its industrial development. Immigrants and migrants, of varied ethnic groups arrived in a city that held no previously established cultural patterns. Each contributed to the social and cultural character of the community. Today's Holyoke is made up of the identities and cultures of all her immigrant and migrant groups that have either settled or passed through her borders.

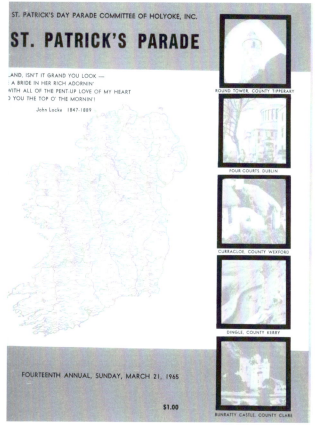

1965 program cover from the St. Patrick's Parade. From the collection of Wistariahurst Museum.

Between 1865 and 1890 Holyoke regularly had a higher percentage of foreign born in its total population than any other city in the state. Even into the 1900s, on Holyoke's streets and in its factories, men and women from Ireland, Great Britain, Canada, Germany, Italy and later Puerto Rico lived and toiled together. They left their homelands and brought with them a distinctive culture that they did not surrender in their new home. Once in Holyoke, each ethnic group staked out a territory and attempted to preserve its cultural heritage while adapting to the strange ways of a new homeland.

An important component of Irish culture in Holyoke was Irish nationalism. Long after they had departed from Ireland, Irish Americans remained preoccupied with the liberation of Ireland from British oppression. A series of campaigns to obtain full political equality created a sense of national identity among the Irish. The famine in Ireland had deepened and transformed these convictions. The Irish recalled the painful deaths of those who perished, but also harbored some shame that they had fled to America and not stayed to avert that catastrophe. Through organizations like the Ancient Order of Hibernians and the Fenians, the Irish were able to embrace their nationalism as well as continue to forge their new home in Holyoke.

Timothy Sullivan, President of the St. Patrick's Parade Committee in 1968 wrote "The Irishman, whether Irish born or Irish by heritage, has long believed that it was the good Saint Patrick who was principally responsible for his individual gift of faith. With this in mind, the Irish and the descendants of the Irish, honor and perpetuate the memory and the spirit of this great and saintly man. Sus-

The Caldonian Band marches past City Hall in the St. Patrick's Parade. Photograph courtesy of the Holyoke Public Library History Room.

Sacred Heart's float in the St. Patrick's Parade. Photograph courtesy of the Wistariahurst Museum Archives.

tained by the profound, yet simple, teachings of Saint Patrick, the Irishman has been able to surmount oppression and depression, has learned to respect his fellow man and his beliefs, share in his hope for the future, and always has he demonstrated his generous loyalty to his adopted country. In this tense and turbulent world of today, with hate, prejudice and fear eating away at the heart and soul of mankind, it is indeed fitting and just that we unite in order to honor God, pay tribute to the memory of Saint Patrick, and salute our truly great and wonderful United States of America."

Though it started as a celebration of Irish heritage, the St. Patrick's Parade in Holyoke has not only become one of the largest in the nation, but also an important cultural institution for the city. Over the years many cultural heritage organizations have joined in the celebration. Daniel C. Boyle has written of the pride he feels when watching the parade: "Along the [St. Patrick's Day] parade route, I can never forget the thousands of marchers, the scores of bands, the high stepping girls, the multitudes which lined the curbs and waved from upstairs windows. The friendly shows…seemed to be coming from an echo chamber…"

One of Holyoke's most famous authors, Mary Doyle Curran, who wrote *Parish on the Hill*, poignantly wrote, "My grandfather spoke the language of his people, though he always spoke it in his own way. He was an Irishman, and twenty years or a million years in America, his roots were still planted as firmly in Ireland as Saint Patrick's."

While the Irish defined themselves by their nationalism, the French Canadians did not seek to create a new Quebec or Montreal in Holyoke. Many French Canadians thought they would return home. French Canadians came to Holyoke chiefly between 1870-1890 with many distinctive ethnic characteristics. Settling for the most part in the wards below the canals, they tended to stay on in their first environment not far from the Railroad station where many of them arrived from Montreal and Quebec. They cherished their language, way of life, and sought to live together in a familiar community that allowed their national, religious, social and ancestral roots to remain strong.

Those who contributed to Holyoke's success in industry, recreation, the service industry or religious organizations seem to retain a certain memory or identity related to Holyoke. Photograph courtesy of the Wistariahurst Museum Archives.

Some French Canadians, however, were in Holyoke to stay. Anita Marcotte Healey remembers that she had "no family in Canada. They're all in Holyoke. We didn't speak French except to my maternal grandmother. She couldn't speak English but did teach herself to speak by listening to the radio."

Though French Canadian immigrants became American citizens in growing numbers, they were slower to claim citizenship than any other ethnic groups. This was due partly to language barriers and partly to the idea that they hoped to return home to Canada. However, the youngest immigrants were the first to make the decision to become citizens. In 1885, for example, 75% of the French Canadians admitted to citizen-

This family hiked to Mount Tom, a memory which lives in the minds of many Holyokers. Photograph courtesy of the Wistariahurst Museum Archives.

ship in Holyoke were 30 years old or younger.

Through the Lutheran Church, the Turnverein and the German Benevolent Society, the Germans were a self sufficient community, enjoying their Kaffeeklatch, and taking pride in their homes with window boxes or gardens. The Lutheran parochial school where children were taught German further encultured German immigrants.

Heritage means many things to many people, and is most often passed down from generation to generation. Heritage is embedded in many things, like food traditions, folktales and storytelling, and music. For example, after an observed Lenten period, Easter is one of the happiest days in Polish families. Easter Eggs are traditionally decorated on Good Friday. On Easter Sunday, there are baskets containing a piece of each of the meats to be eaten at breakfast. The Easter bread, salt, butter and horseradish are separated into containers and packed into decorated baskets. These baskets were taken to church to receive the priest's blessing. Every half hour the priest walks down the aisle of church and the baskets are uncovered and blessed. The foods are then taken home and returned to their place on the buffet. Traditionally the meal is an open house, with friends and family invited. Guests are greeted by the hostess, who offers a wedge of hard boiled egg and wishes them a year of good health and happiness. Americans of Polish descent celebrate Wigilia, or Christmas Eve. This holiday combines the somberness of advent with joyousness of the season. The tradition dictates that the meal begins when the first star appears in the sky. Family and friends gather around the dinner table to break Oplatek, or a blessed wafer. The eldest member of the family offers the wafer to an adjacent person, who in turn passes the wafer on. Following dinner, the group attends Midnight Mass. Polish families are known to cook up kielbasa, borscht, golompkis, babka (bread), pierogi and kapusta. Polish traditions are continued in many ways, especially in Holyoke and neighboring Chicopee, where many former Holyokers now live. Gramps Restaurant on Lyman Street still serves traditionally Polish food.

In the Italian tradition during Christmas, there would often be the smell of baked goods wafting from the kitchen. Grandparents were honored with special roles in Christmas festivities. Christmas Eve dinner, a meatless meal, would be followed by games, tasting pastries and liquors in people's homes, while the women stayed at home to prepare the next day's dinner, usually served in mid afternoon. Grandparents attended Midnight Mass while their children remained home to fix a midnight snack to eat upon their arrival. It is at this festive meal that presents would be opened. Most would stay up until dawn and be up again for 9 AM Mass the next morning. Other fine cuisine from the Italian heritage includes linguini, stuffed peppers and espresso.

German traditional preparations were the same as practiced in Germany. Instead of hunting boar as was tradition in Germany, however, the prey in America became deer or pheasant. Hunting parties, consisting of three generations of men, rose before dawn to hunt. They hunted in West Holyoke where deer ate apples in the orchards. They would return home to a family dinner, and after that, play pinochle until the wee hours of the night.

The Reyes Family, photograph taken in 1979. They are Judith, 17, Dennis, 13, Anna West, 20, Joel, 8, and Aida Reyes in the back. Photograph courtesy of the Holyoke Public Library History Room.

126

A French Canadian Christmas can begin with Midnight Mass. Following the service, families gathered together for reveillons, the traditional supper. The main course is usually a tourtiere, or a meat pie, with desert being buche de noel. When supper was over there was an exchange of small gifts. Folktales and storytelling were an important part of French Canadian life. Recited by parents as bedtime stories or by a memere or pepere to amuse their grandchildren, these wonderful tales are also appreciated by adults.

Cecile Barthello, French Canadian, believes she understands what new immigrants and migrants are faced with when they enter Holyoke: "I understand the ones who are minority groups we felt that at first – we could not speak English fluently….but we had to learn it in school. And we did write it better than we spoke it. …..I understand other people who cannot express themselves …. We suffered a lot, because we could have had much better jobs."

An anonymous Puerto Rican simply stated "…No matter where I am, here in the U.S. or in my own island, Puerto Rico, I don't deny my language because it is beautiful like music….My traditions are different and because of these I am classified as Hispanic. The art, folklore, music (danga and plena), the native cuisine are different, our custom of sharing, our brotherhood bring us together. For all of these, I am very proud."

Gil Sotolongo, of Puerto Rican descent, has said about the problems facing the new wave of migrants to Holyoke, "This town was here before we even got here, and they had a lot of the same kinds of problems. If it wasn't the Puerto Ricans, it was the Irish, the French, the Polish, and slowly but surely, its still there….There's a lot of bigotry, but I think we are breaking down those barriers…. After a while, your neighbors get to know you, and I think that is the only way we are going to break down those barriers. Maria Roche and her husband Carlos migrated from Puerto Rico in 1976. Both found work in local tobacco fields when they first moved to the area. Carlos then found work at a foundry. Maria continues to cling to her heritage by practicing Puerto Rican holiday traditions, but also said "I was born in Puerto Rico and I like it better there. I love its climate, which has no comparison."

Popular Puerto Rican foods include pork, rice, fried plantains and flan (custard). Local restaurants like Fernandes Family Restaurant cater to the needs of the Puerto Rican community with these traditional foods.

Vejigante masks are an important facet of Puerto Rican culture. Each main Carnival in Puerto Rico has its unique Vejigante character. For example, the Fiestas de Hatillo, which is a town in Puerto Rico, commemorate the death of the Innocent Saints. The masks for this celebration are made with colored metal strings. In a Carnival in Loiza, masks are made from coconut shells and are decorated with bright colors

A sign advertising only a few of the points of interest in Holyoke. Photograph courtesy of the Wistariahurst Museum Archives.

and horns. The idea is to have the good vejigantes get rid of the evil ones through the native dance of bomba y plena. Before going to bed on January 5, Puerto Rican children would cut grass and place it under their beds. During the night, it was believed that the Three Kings would bring them gifts. The grass is for the camels, who must carry the presents to the children.

Jaime Iglesia, born in Puerto Rico, enjoys his work at Nuestras Raices. He says, "I integrate my Puerto Rican culture into my life by working with other communities, especially with the Latino Community. I say 'Latino' because we all share the enjoyment of working together as a whole."

Jesse Maceo Vega-Frey, a native of Holyoke, explains the connection and isolation sometimes felt in Holyoke: "Having one Latino parent and one white parent would be a tricky endeavor anywhere but in Holyoke, where the lines between those worlds is so divided, the balancing of those two realities has always been a

128

There are remnants of Holyoke's industries that remain in Holyoke today. These examples are of Holyoke Screw Company and J.W. Jolley.

complicated line to walk. Add to that a non-religious and politically radical upbringing, an Ecuadorian – not Puerto Rican- dad and a non-Irish mom from Ohio, well, I didn't fit squarely into any of the boxes laid out before me. This identity I've grown up with has resulted in feeling a deep connection to Holyoke and all its communities as well as a deep isolation from them at the same time. In truth, I feel like I can hold and embody all the dynamics at play in this city in my own life, in my own body, and in my own mind and flow – or stumble – between them with some degree of integrity and grace. I think this dance between connection and isolation, between belonging and alienation, has everything to do with my artwork. This city and my relationship to it continues to be a fundamental driving force of my creative endeavors."

Michael Sullivan (Mayor of Holyoke 2000 - present) believes "Holyoke is a stronger community for having different cultures."

One looks around Holyoke today and sees glimpses of Holyoke's industrial past. This fading sign on the side of an apartment building is just one of those windows into our past. However, there is much to look forward to in Holyoke's future, with its cultural diversity and its mosaic of identities. Photograph courtesy of the Holyoke Public Library History Room.

Holyoke Timeline

1684   John Riley purchased 16 acres of land on what would be known as Ireland Parish

1786   Ireland Parish was made a separate parish of West Springfield

1799   The First Congregational Society of Ireland Parish was organized; services held in meeting house

1803   First Baptist Society of Ireland Parish organized

1831   Ireland Parish had 130 dwellings

1832   The Hadley Falls Company was incorporated

1842   The Connecticut River Railroad received a charter to build a railroad line from Chicopee to Northampton by way of South Hadley Falls to meet the Hartford and Springfield Railroad

1845   March 21. The Connecticut River Railroad was allowed to change the route of the railroad line to cross the river at Willimansett and run through Ireland Parish to Northampton

1845   December 13. First train on the Connecticut River Railroad line from Springfield to Northampton passed through the area of Ireland Parish which would become known as Ireland Depot

1846   George C. Ewing of the Fairbanks & Company scalemakers of St. Johnsbury, Vermont, received the commission to acquire land and water rights at Ireland Parish for a group of Boston financiers

1846   Potato famine in Ireland

1847   March. George C. Ewing purchased the first 37 acres of land in Ireland Parish. He would eventually purchase a total of 1,100 acres of land, a stone quarry at the foot of Mount Tom, the controlling interest in the "Proprietors of Locks and Canals"

1847   June. The Hadley Falls Company, which had been incorporated in 1832 to build a cotton mill, released its name for the new company that would develop at Ireland Parish

1847   July 8. Water survey began to measure the river at South Hadley Falls. The findings showed the flow at 6,980 cubic feet per second with a fall of 60 feet – the equivalent of 30,000 horsepower or 550 mill powers (largest mill at the time used 4 or 5 mill powers) – the greatest potential for mill development in New England

1847   Thanksgiving Day. The last steamboat passed through the South Hadley Canal, a navigational canal which had been built in 1792 to convey boats around the falls

1847   December 6. First stone laid for the canals of the Hadley Falls Company at Ireland Parish

1848   January 1. Start of a strike among the Irish day laborers working on the canals after their wages were cut from 75 cents to 70 cents per day

1848   January. The property purchased by George C. Ewing passed into the hands of the Hadley Falls Company

1848   February 4. The first stone was laid for the foundation of 32 tenements being built by the Hadley Falls Company for its workers

1848   April 29. Chicopee incorporated as a town from part of Springfield

1848   August 5. There were 1,277 men employed by the Hadley Falls Company building the dam and canals. "The Patch" was created just above the dam site by the workers and their families

1848   November 18. First dam across the Connecticut completed and washed away – "you're old dam's gone to hell by way of Willimansett"

1849   April. Work on the new dam began

1849   September. Hampden Freeman began publishing every Friday

1849   Second Congregational Society of Ireland Depot organized with 20 members; first church built on Dwight Street (corner High) in 1852; replaced by church on Maple Street (corner Appleton)

dedicated in January 1885; partly destroyed by fire in 1919; church rebuilt and rededicated December 1921

1849   Second Baptist Society of Ireland Depot organized

1849   October 16. Water from the river above the dam was pumped into the new 3,000,000 gallon reservoir which was bounded by Lyman, Maple, Fountain and High Streets

1849   October 22. New dam, 80 feet wide and 1,000 feet long, completed. Water power estimates at the time calculated that it could power 1,200,000 spindles and employ 100,000 persons

1850   Farming was the chief occupation in Hampden County.

1850   Holyoke incorporated as a town

1852   Springfield incorporated as a city

1853   Parson's Paper Mill organized

1853   First Methodist Society organized

1854   January. Lyman Cotton Mills established

1855   Holyoke's population was 4,639 (2,623 native born and 1,657 Irish); the town had 514 dwellings for 778 families

1855   Parsons Paper began to manufacture paper

1856   Holyoke established a Board of Health

1856   St. Jerome's Roman Catholic parish (Irish) established

1857   Hadley Falls Company declared bankruptcy

1859   The Holyoke Water Power Company assumed control of all of the holdings of the Hadley Falls Company, including the dams and canals, the stone quarry and the swing ferry

1860	Importation of the first French Canadians to Holyoke
1860	There were 536 dwellings for Holyoke's 4,997 inhabitants
1861	Civil War began. 250 Holyokers served in the war and 40 were lost
1863	St. Paul's Episcopal Society established
1863	The Holyoke Water Power Company began to lease sites for non-textile ventures.
1863	The Holyoke Mirror, sucessor to the Hampden Freeman, was sold to Burt and Lyman of Springfield and the name was changed to the Transcript
1865	Civil War ends
1865	Merrick Thread Mill and Germania Mills established; Whiting Paper Company established
1865	Holyoke's population was 5,648. The percentage of foreign born (43%) was greater than any other town in the state
1866	The Holyoke Board of Health reported it found one block on High Street with 17 rooms housing 105 persons
1867	Evangelical Lutheran Society organized; first church on Jackson Street built 1867
1867	Massachusetts law passed stating that all children under the age of 15 must go to school at least three months a year
1868	Sisters of Notre Dame establish a school in St. Jerome's parish
1869	Precious Blood Roman Catholic parish (French) formed; church on Cabot Street dedicated January 1870; destroyed by fire May 1875; new church dedicated June 1878 (demolished 1987)
1869	The 11 paper mills in Holyoke produced 30 tons of paper per day

1869   Abortive Fenian invasion of Canada embarrasses Irish community

1870   Holyoke had 1,848 dwellings for its 10,733 inhabitants (5,257 native born; 2,850 Irish; and 1,731 French Canadian)

1870   Roman Catholic Diocese of Springfield established, from part of Boston

1871   Holyoke's town hall construction begun

1872   Town of Holyoke took Ashley and Wright ponds to supply fresh water for its residents; the reservoir on High Street used since 1849 was then dismantled

1872   The Holyoke Lumber Company held its first log drive on the Connecticut River bringing 15,000,000 logs downriver

1872   Bridge to South Hadley Falls constructed

1873   Holyoke incorporated as a city

1873   The 14 paper mills in Holyoke were producing 48 tons of paper per day. The E.T. Bosworth Company was employing 300 persons making 10,000,000 bricks a year

1873   Smallpox epidemic in Holyoke

1874   Holyoke had 14 paper mills employing 2,000 workers, 3 cotton mills employing 1,900 workers, 2 thread mills employing 800, 3 woolen mills employing 450, and the Holyoke Machine Works employing 250

1874   Farr Alpaca Company and William Skinner's Silk Mill established at Holyoke

1875   Holyoke's population was 16,260

1875   Precious Blood Church burned

1875   French Catholic Cemetery (now Precious Blood) on the Granby Plains in South Hadley dedicated

1876   City Hall dedicated

1877   Providence Hospital opened

1878   Sacred Heart Roman Catholic (Irish) parish formed from part of St. Jerome's

1878   Holyoke's Opera House opens

1878   New Precious Blood Church completed

1880   Holyoke had a population of 21,915 (4,368 native born; 4,241 Irish; 4,902 French Canadian; 509 German); an average of 10.52 persons per dwelling

1883   Holyoke was the "greatest paper-making center in the world" with 20 mills producing 177 tons daily. By 1892, Holyoke was producing 1/20 of all the paper manufactured in the United States

1884   Holyoke Street Railway incorporated

1884   The Knights of Labor was organized in Holyoke by machine tenders and beater engineers

1885   First Presbyterian Society organized

1885   Textile workers led by German immigrants strike at Germania mills and Skinner Silk Mills

1886   Highlands Methodist Episcopal Church dedicated

1886   Our Lady of the Rosary Roman Catholic parish (French) formed

1887   First Congregational Church built on Pleasant Street

1888   Loomis and Dwight purchase the Transcript

1890   Perpetual Help Roman Catholic parish (French) formed from part of Precious Blood; church and school on Maple Street dedicated 1891; new church dedicated 1923 (destroyed by fire 1999)

1890   Holyoke had a population of 35,637 (5,993 Irish; 7,046 French Canadian; 1,455 German); Americans born of native parentage was only 17% of the population; foreign born accounted for almost 48% of the population.

1890   YMCA opened

1890   Holyoke had 5 woolen mills employing 1,048; 5 cotton mills employing 2,989; 20 paper mills employing 3,260; and 13 foundries and machine shops employing 837 workers

1893   Holyoke Hospital opened

1893   Kocziusczko Club organized

1893   Holyoke's International Brotherhood of Papermakers won its national charter from the American Federation of Labor

1894   Grace Congregational Society organized

1894   Holyoke had 24 paper manufacturers (fine writing, Bristol board, manila, wrapping, book paper, glazed paper, carpet linings, ledger paper), 3 envelope manufacturers, 2 cotton mills, 1 hosiery manufacturer, 1 dyer, 2 silk mills, 2 thread mills, 5 woolen mills, 16 machinery manufacturers (wire, tools, turbines, cutlery, iron foundry, boilers, paper mill machinery, hydrants, blacksmith works, bicycles, steam engines), and 19 miscellaneous manufacturers (trolley tracks, lumber, bricks, dandy rolls, fourdrainer sires, lead pipe, valves, carriages & wagons, wire cloth, steam & gas pipes, leather belting, paper rulers, & etc.)

1895   Mountain Park opened as a Trolley Park

1896   Appointment of first Polish priest

1899   Albert Steiger built his new store on High Street.

1899   American Writing Paper Company is formed

1900   Holyoke had a population of 45,712 with an average of 10.9 persons per dwelling. Only 17% of the population was native born of native parentage; 42% were native born of foreign parentage;

and 41% foreign born (Irish 5,650; French Canadian 6,991; British 2,945; German 1,757; Polish/Russian 1,126; other 492)

1900	Italian Progressive Society formed
1900	Holy Family Roman Catholic parish formed
1900	Mater Dolorosa Roman Catholic parish (Polish) formed
1902	City of Holyoke took over the gas and electric lighting plants from the Holyoke Water Power Company and established the Holyoke Gas & Electric
1902	New Public Library opened; first librarian Miss Sarah Ely, retired
1902	Skinner Coffee House opened for working women of Holyoke
1903	Immaculate Conception Roman Catholic parish (French) formed
1903	One-half of Holyoke's population was of French descent
1905	Holy Cross Roman Catholic parish (Irish) formed
1910	American Writing Paper loses control of the paper market
1910	The foreign born population in Holyoke jumps to 23,238 from 18,921
1912	Skinner Memorial Chapel added to the Second Congregational Church
1913	Blessed Sacrament Roman Catholic parish formed
1915	Connecticut Valley Lumber Company makes its last log drive
1917	Greek Orthodox parish formed; church dedicated.
1917	Holyoke's peak population was reached with 62,210 persons

1917   The Jones Act makes the people of Puerto Rico citizens of the United States

1920   Census for Holyoke documents that 33.6% of the total population is foreign born

1921   Girl Scouts of Holyoke receive their charter

1923   American Writing Paper declares bankruptcy

1927   Lyman Cotton Mills closed

1930   Holyoke's foreign born population drops to 28.7% of the total population

1932   Junior League of Holyoke founded

1934   Germania Mills is reorganized and assumes new name of Livingston Worsted Mills

1934   National Textile Strike. Eventually more than 3,500 textile workers in Holyoke will be picketing

1940   Holyoke's foreign born population drops to 22.4% of the total population

1940s   The City begins developing a new power source - hydro electro power

1946   Holyoke Graduate School founded

1947   Holyoke Graduate School changes name to Holyoke Junior College

1949   Music Department at the Holyoke Public Library opens under Miss Vivian Borque; patrons could borrow music recordings

1954   Operation Wetback

1956   Hungarian Revolution in Hungary

1957   Barowsky's Lestoil becomes more than a household name throughout the nation; it is the most advertised product on television

1959 Skinner mansion, Wistariahurst, donated to the City of Holyoke

1960 100 Spanish speaking people live in Holyoke

1964 Holyoke Junior College becomes Holyoke Community College; classes are held at Elmwood

1968 Economic recession on the Island of Puerto Rico results in influx of Puerto Ricans to the city seeking employment in the tobacco industry

1970 2,000 Spanish speaking people live in Holyoke

1971 Holyoke Community College breaks new ground at Homestead Avenue

1976 The City of Holyoke celebrates its bicentennial

1978 The Volleyball Hall of Fame, Inc. formed for the purpose of establishing and maintaining a living memorial to the sport of volleyball

1979 Holyoke Mall at Ingleside built

1980 William Skinner Mill burns to the ground

1982 Nueva Esperanza, Inc. founded in Holyoke to facilitate economic development

1987 Mountain Park closed

1989 Nueva Esperanza, Inc. leases the Skinner Coffee House

1993 Carousel moved to Heritage State Park

2005 Parsons Paper closed

2006 Luchini's family restaurant closes as a legend in Holyoke, after 103 years

Resources

Primary Sources

American International College, Springfield, Massachusetts.
   Oral History Collection.

Heritage State Park, Holyoke, Massachusetts
   Photograph Collection.

Holyoke Public Library History Room, Holyoke, Massachusetts
   Local Files.
   Photograph Files.

Wistariahurst Museum, Holyoke, Massachusetts
   Holyoke Collection.
   Skinner Family Collection.
   Taped Interviews and Archival Material on Skinner Mill Employees; Oral histories collected 1989, by
      Emelie Plourde for Smith College project.

Holyoke *Transcript-Telegram*

Government Documents

U.S. Census Manuscript Population Schedules.
   Seventh Census (1850), Hampden County, Massachusetts.
   Eighth Census (1860), Hampden County, Massachusetts.
   Ninth Census (1870), Hampden County, Massachusetts.
   Tenth Census (1880), Hampden County, Massachusetts.
   Eleventh Census (1890), Hampden County, Massachusetts.
   Twelveth Census (1900), Hampden County, Massachusetts.
   Thirteenth Census (1910), Hampden County, Massachusetts.
   Fourteenth Census (1920), Hampden County, Massachusetts.
   Fifteenth Census (1930), Hampden County, Massachusetts.
   Sixteenth Census (1940), Hampden County, Massachusetts.
   Seventeenth Census (1950), Hampden County, Massachusetts.
   Eighteenth Census (1960), Hampden County, Massachusetts.
   Nineteenth Census (1970), Hampden County, Massachusetts.
   Twentieth Census (1980), Hampden County, Massachusetts.
   Twenty-first Census (1990), Hampden County, Massachusetts.
   Twenth-second Census (2000), Hampden County, Massachusetts.

Holyoke, Massachusetts. *Municipal Register.* 1874-1940.

Holyoke, Massachusetts. *Town Report.* 1851-1870.

Holyoke, Massachusetts. *Holyoke City Directory.* 1890-1990.

Massachusetts Bureau of Statistics and Labor. *Bulletin.* Boston, 1897-1905.

Secondary Sources
The American Immigrant, An Illustrated History. New York, N.Y.: Time Inc., Life Books, 2004

Bode, Janet. *New Kids in Town: Oral Histories of Immigrant Teens.* New York, NY.: Scholastic Incorporated, 1989.

Bodnar, John. *Immigration and Industrialization: Ethnicity in an American Mill Town, 1870-1940.* Pittsburgh: University
of Pittsburgh Press, 1977.

Brault, Gerald J. *The French-Canadian Heritage in New England.* Hanover, N.H.: University Press of New England,
1986.

Brisenden, Paul F. *Earnings of Factory Workers, 1899-1927.* Washington, D.C.: Census Monograph, 1929.

Brown, Richard D. *Modernization: The Transformation of American Life 1600-1865.* Illinois: Hill and Wang, 1976.

Byrne, Stephen. *Irish Emigration to the United States: What It Has Been and What It Is.* New York: The Catholic
Publication Society, 1874.

Coan, Peter Morton. *Ellis Island Interviews: Immigrants Tell Their Stories in Their Own Words.* New York, N.Y.: Barnes
& Nobles, Inc., 1987.

Curran, Mary Doyle. *The Parish and the Hill.* Boston: Houghton Mifflin, 1948.

Czitrom, Daniel. "The Hidden Holyoke: An Historical Introduction, 1870-1940." Unpublished manuscript,
Mount Holyoke College.

Dalzell, Robert F. Jr. *Enterprising Elite: The Boston Associates and the World They Made.* New York, NY: W.W. and
Norton Co., 1987.

Dawson, Devon. *Holyoke.(Postcard History Series).* Portsmouth, N.H.: Arcadia Publishing. 2004.

142

Della Penna, Craig V. *Holyoke*. Portsmouth, N.H.: Arcadia Publishing. 1997.

Devino, W. Stanley, et al. *A Study of Textile Mill Closings in Selected New England Communities*. Orono: University of Maine Press, 1966.

Doane, Frank H. *History of Holyoke, Massachusetts from 1830-1870*. Unpublished manuscript, Holyoke Public Library.

Drudy, P.J. In *The Irish in America: Emigration, Assimilation, and Impact*. Cambridge, Eng.: Cambridge University Press, 1985.

Dubovik, Paul N. "Housing in Holyoke and its Effects on Family Life, 1860-1910." *Historical Journal of Western Massachusetts* 4(1975): 40-50.

Moraga, Ricardo, Randi Silnutzer, Roger Tinchnell, and Katie Tolles. *Folk Heritage and the Arts in Holyoke*. Holyoke, M.A.: Holyoke Public Schools, 1985.

Gabriel, Ralph H. *The Founding of Holyoke, 1848*. Princeton: Princeton University Press, 1936.

Greene, Constance McLaughlin. *Holyoke Massachusetts: A Case History of the Industrial Revolution in America*. Yale University Press, 1939.

Gonzales, Juan. *Harvest of Empire. A History of Latinos in America*. New York, NY: Viking Penguin, 2000.

Hachey, Thomas E., Joseph M. Hernon, Jr., and Lawrence J. McCaffrey. *The Irish Experience*. New Jersey: Prentiss-Hall, 1989.

Harper, Wyatt E. *The Story of Holyoke*. Not published. 1973.

Hartford, William F. *Paper City: Class Development in Holyoke, Massachusetts, 1850-1920*. Ph.D. diss., University of Massachusetts Amherst, 1983.

Haebler, Peter. *Habitants in Holyoke: The Development of the French Canadian Community in a Massachusetts City, 1865 1910*. Ph.D. diss., University of New Hampshire, 1976.

Ignatiev, Noel. *How the Irish Became White*. New York, NY: Routledge, 1995.

Kennedy, Robert E. *The Irish: Emigration, Marriage, and Fertility*. Berkeley: University of California Press, 1973.

MacDonald, William. "The French Canadians in New England." *Quarterly Journal of Economics* 12 (April 1898): 245-279.

Massachsuetts Industries. International Publishing Company Publishers, 1886.

McCaffrey, Lawrence J. *The Irish Diaspora in America.* Bloomington: Indiana University Press, 1976.

Meagher, Timothy J. ed. *From Paddy to Studs: Irish-American Communities in the Turn of the Century Era, 1880-1910.* Westport, Conn.: Greenwood Press, 1986.

Merkel DiCarlo, Ella. *Holyoke-Chicopee: A Perspective.* Transcript Telegram. Book Press Brattleboro, VT, 1982.

Morgan, Myfanwy, and Hilda H. Golden. "Immigrant Families in an Industrial City: A Study of Households in Holyoke." *Journal of Family History* 4 (Spring): 59-68.

Morrison, Joan and Charlotte Fox Zabusky. *American Mosaic: The Immigrant Experience in the Words of Those Who Lived It.* Pittsburg: University of Pittsburg Press, 1980.

Namias, June. *First Generation: In the Words of Twentieth-Century American Immigrants.* Illinois: University of Illinois Press, 1992.

Osgood, Reverend G.C. *Story of the Holyoke Churches.* Holyoke, M.A.: Transcript Publishing Company, 1890.

Pedulla, Marianne. "Labor in a City of Immigrants: Holyoke, 1882-1888." *Historical Journal of Massachusetts* 13 (1985): 147-161.

Petrin, Ronald A. "Culture, Community, and Politics: French-Canadians in Massachusetts, 1885-1915". In *The Little Canadas of New England*, edited by Claire Quintal. Worcester, Mass.: French Institute/Assumption College, 1983.

Rosado-Merced, Xenia. "Where in the World is Puerto Rico?" *Spanish Translations*, 2001.

Rosenzweig, Roy. *Eight Hours for What We Will: Workers and Leisure in an Industrial City, 1870-1920.* Cambridge, Eng.: Cambridge University Press, 1983.

The Story of Holyoke, Massachusetts in Painting and in Prose. Holyoke Public Library, 1954.

Saxon, Bruce. "Fall River and the Decline of the New England Textile Industry, 1949-1954." *Historical Journal of Massachusetts* 16 (1988): 54-74.

Sylvester, Nathaniel Bartlett. *History of the Connecticut River Valley in MA*. Philadelphia: Louis H. Everts, 1879.

Thibodeau, Kate Navarra. *Holyoke: The Skinner Family and Wistariahurst*. Portsmouth, NH: Arcadia Publishing, 2006.

Ueda, Reed. *Postwar Immigrant America: A Social History*. Bedford Books of St. Martins Press, 1994.

Underwood, Kenneth Wilson. *Protestant and Catholic: Religious and Social Interaction in an Industrial Community*. 1957. Reprint. Westport, Conn.: Greenwood Press, 1973.

Walker, Mack. *Germany and the Emigration, 1816-1885*. Cambridge: Harvard University Press, 1964.

Woodham-Smith, Cecil. *The Great Hunger: Ireland, 1845-1849*. New York: Harper and Row, 1962.

Wright, Harry A. *Indian Deeds of Hampden County*. Springfield, 1911.